Performance Cultures and Doped Bodies

Challenging Categories, Gender Norms, and Policy Responses

Jesper Andreasson
April Henning

Performance Cultures and Doped Bodies

Challenging Categories, Gender Norms, and Policy Responses

Jesper Andreasson
April Henning

First published in 2021
as part of the *Sport and Society* Book Imprint
doi:10.18848/978-1-86335-242-0/CGP (Full Book)

Common Ground Research Networks
60 Hazelwood Dr.
University of Illinois Research Park
Champaign, IL
61820

Library of Congress Cataloging-in-Publication Data

Names: Andreasson, Jesper, author. | Henning, April, author.
Title: Performance cultures and doped bodies : challenging categories, gender norms, and policy responses / Jesper Andreasson, April Henning.
Description: Champaign, IL : Common Ground, [2021] | Includes bibliographical references. | Summary: "Building on data gathered through ethnographic fieldwork, studies of online doping communities, and in-depth case studies, this book embraces the challenge of moving beyond traditional and historical doping dichotomies - such as sport or fitness, online or offline, pleasure or harm, masculinity or femininity, and health or harm - and develops new terminology to understand trajectories to and from doping"-- Provided by publisher.
Identifiers: LCCN 2021014514 (print) | LCCN 2021014515 (ebook) | ISBN 9780949313997 (hardback) | ISBN 9781863352413 (paperback) | ISBN 9781863352420 (adobe pdf)
Subjects: LCSH: Doping in sports--Social aspects. | Athletes--Drug use. | Human body--Social aspects. | Physical fitness--Social aspects. | Gender identity in sports.
Classification: LCC RC1230 .A533 2021 (print) | LCC RC1230 (ebook) | DDC 362.29088/796--dc23
LC record available at https://lccn.loc.gov/2021014514
LC ebook record available at https://lccn.loc.gov/2021014515

Cover Photo Credit: cellar-door/depositphotos.com

Table of Contents

Preface and Acknowledgements i

Chapter 1 1
Introduction

Chapter 2 13
The Interwoven Histories of Sports and Fitness Doping

Chapter 3 29
Trajectories, Cultural Recalibration, and Contextual Mobility

Chapter 4 43
Women's Gender-Bending in Man-Spreading Cultures

Chapter 5 59
Sex, Drugs, and Muscles: "Welcome to Planet Porno"

Chapter 6 73
Anti-Doping: Producing Health or Harm?

Chapter 7 91
Conclusions

Appendix: Methods and Data 99

Preface and Acknowledgements

This book is the result of a collaboration that started when the two authors met at a conference organized in Aarhus, Denmark, by the International Network for Doping Researchers (INDR) in 2015. Here a relatively small group of about 40 scholars within the field of doping research, mostly but not exclusively in the social sciences, gathered to present new research and to find inspiration for future projects. By chance, we ended up talking at lunch after one of the conference sessions. We soon realized that we shared an interest in sociological perspectives and ways of conceptualizing doping practices and preventative incentives. The contexts of our research focus were quite different, though. Whereas one of us (Jesper) had mainly focused on ethnographic fieldwork and drug use practices in gym and fitness environments (interviewing and observing fitness enthusiasts, personal trainers, bodybuilders, and others), the other (April) was more at home and familiar with doping in the sports context, focusing on health and policy implications for athletes (historical and contemporary) in relation to the World Anti-Doping Agency (WADA).

Although we initially considered these two contexts as more or less unrelated, in a similar manner to how scholars in general have tended to see them, it gradually became obvious that our research experiences, fieldwork, and data analyses overlapped. Discussing our understandings of data we had collected over the years made it clear that those with hands-on, practical experience of doping often operated in diverse and parallel doping contexts simultaneously. Since then we have written a handful of articles together, gradually establishing a common understanding and platform for our collaboration. This all led up to the idea for this book, in which we try to at least partially rethink the dominant ways of contextualizing doping as a question of "either/or." Rather, we understand it as one of "both/and." Like smudging lines drawn by a pencil, this book is the result of our ambition to call into question the hegemonic and almost mandatory separations prominent in doping research and manifested in separations between different doping contexts and perspectives, such as sports/fitness, online/offline, and prevention/harm reduction, to mention a few.

We are grateful that Jörg Krieger at the Department of Public Health, Aarhus University, and Kerry Dixon at Common Ground, liked the idea for this project and gave us the opportunity to publish this book. We are also greatful for the feedback and encouragement that Jörg and Matthew Dunn from Deakin University, Australia, provided in reading the manuscript as a whole. Thanks. We would also like to express our gratitude to *the Swedish Research Council for Health, Working Life and Welfare (FORTE)* for financial support.

Thanks also to the following friends and scholars for valuable input and inspiration: Paul Dimeo at the University of Stirling and Thomas Johansson at the

University of Gothenburg provided insights on both historical and contemporary challenges and developments for this manuscript. John Campbell also gave us feedback and information on the U.K.'s harm reduction efforts, as did Johan Öhman who works with doping prevention in Sweden. We would also like to thank Ellen Sverkersson at Linnaeus University for providing novel ideas and new understandings of the changing demography of doping, particularly women's fitness doping. Finally, of course, we are sincerely grateful for all those who have generously shared their experiences and thoughts about doping during fieldwork. Thank you.

Some of the chapters in this book build on articles already published by the authors in journals including *Drugs: Education, Prevention and Policy; Communication & Sport; Journal of Bodies, Sexualities, and Masculinites;* and *Sport in Society.* The text has, however, been adapted to suit the overall idea and framework of the book. As part of this adaptation, data has been re-structured and sometimes re-analyzed.

As this book is the outcome of a joint and mutual collaboration, the author order is alphabetical.

Jesper Andreasson, Kalmar, Sweden
April Henning, Stirling, Scotland

Chapter 1

Introduction

There are, of course, numerous potential explanations for why a person may choose (or not) to use image and performance enhancing drugs (IPEDs), such as anabolic-androgenic steroids (hereafter: steroids) or human growth hormones (hGH). The complexity of engaging as well as disengaging in this activity is most certainly not one dimensional. Instead, it must be understood as something that develops over time, sometimes as a gradual and contingent process. The path that a body/individual follows across space and over the course of time – the doping trajectory and experiences attached to it – can direct our attention to and be traced back to previous experiences, such as physical exercise and situations in which doping was addressed, perhaps in a preventative discussion with parents or in an encouraging manner with friends. Previous experiences then linger and influence current choices and understandings in the "here and now." As such, accounts of the past could be said to echo into the present, which gives bodies, identities, and lifestyles a certain direction to some extent, through their own *sedimented histories* (Ahmed, 2006; Lloyd & Moore, 2015). At the same time, we are not bound by experience. Previous understandings are there but they are also rethought and reconceptualized as new experiences are had or circumstances change. Thus, our histories are not literally sedimented or deterministic. A trajectory can also take its form in relation to something sought-after, in terms of ambitions, ideals, and accomplishments, and with a directionality and gaze towards an imagined future. In short, doping triggers and trajectories involve both histories and a sense of momentum; of motion and the tracing of bodies and identities as they, over time, move from/between certain places, cultures, or contexts in certain "directions." The interplay between history and momentum is an idea that we will return to throughout this book.

Traditionally and historically, doping and how this practice/phenomenon has been approached by scholars largely has come to foreground one of two things: *gender* and/or *context*. In terms of gender, for example, the cultural history of IPED use and the values, bodies, and performances that have been sought and promoted through doping essentially have been analyzed as a question of men and muscular masculinities (Klein, 1993; Christiansen, 2020). Even wider, (doped) muscles and masculinities historically have been connected to warfare and the formation of nations, thus a question of men defending the honour of states, women, and children. In doping research this explanatory logic and narrative has played out in a plethora of studies in which scholars have focused on and analyzed men and their doping practices, stretching over decades and focusing different sports and cultural contexts.

As doping research has centered men and masculinities, analyzing and approaching the practice more or less exclusively as a male and homosocial enterprise, it is not surprising that women's voices historically have been backgrounded in comparison, and thus overshadowed by a (intended or unintended) misogynistic discourse (Andreasson & Johansson, 2020). But times are changing, as has the cultural control that masculinity has held over history and doped bodies (cf. Felski, 1995). Since the turn of the century we have seen how the notion of gym and fitness culture has shifted from that of a male-dominated and subcultural spatiality and enterprise, turning into a more inclusive and gender-neutral conception of how to exercise, diet, and train the body. Women have gradually been included, and the female body ideal has shifted from slim and skinny to that of a toned, athletic, fit, and strong physique, representing cultural ideals, values, and lifestyles that historically have been associated exclusively with masculinity (Boepple et al., 2016). Perhaps unsurprisingly, along with these transformations and conceptualizations of female muscularity and performance cultures, there have also been gradual changes in who engages in IPED use (and whose voices are listened to in research). Similar trends pointing towards processes of destabilization and relocation of how doping has been understood and analyzed in the fitness context can also be seen within the sport context.

Regarding *contexts*, the second bulletpoint foregrounded in doping research, it can be noted that users, policymakers, and stakeholders within sports and the gym and fitness industry, all have taken somewhat different approaches to understand and make meaning of doping. The question of cultural context has also had a huge impact on how current anti-doping policies, preventative work, and harm reduction strategies have played out within various performance cultures. One of the clearest separations between contexts concerns doping in formally governed competitions in (elite) sports (i.e., *sports doping*) and doping as a public health issue – that is, as a social problem predominantly connected to gyms and fitness (i.e., *fitness doping*). Sport and fitness are two broad types of performance cultures that each have their own competitive and/or aesthetic logics, trends, values. At the same time, these current distinctions are not historically immutable, as suggested by Dimeo (2007). Both in research and at a government level, doping was discussed and debated, for example, in terms of usefulness at work and during war time until the 1960s. Additionally, Waddington and Smith (2009) argued that it was not until the introduction of anti-doping rules in sports that this practice became unacceptable (we will return to the cultural and contextual history of fitness/sports doping in chapter 2).

Rigid differentiations between doping contexts and cultures (such as between notions of masculinity and femininity) may be fallacious. As noted above, in this book we argue that understanding doping practices and experiences is seldom a question of either/or, in terms of something that can be culturally/contextually pinpointed or nailed down over time. Rather, doping is a question of both/and: as something taking place in the liminal space and interfaces between (cultural) contexts (such as sports/fitness; online/offline). Here, we use the notion of between contexts in two ways: doping as a *practice* that is done and experienced between contexts (or in parallel contexts simultaneously); and doping as a *phenomenon* that occurs and is given meaning relationally between contexts. In terms of the former, we consider how users' experiences are often not bound to a singular context and the hegemonic ideals and cultural values found there. Instead, individuals weave between and move across various settings in their trajectories to and from doping, as goals and lifestyles change over time. This requires us to look beyond traditional dividing lines into the contextual between spaces where values, perspectives, and practices may be reformed. Approaching the "between" also allows us to consider doping as a phenomenon in a more dynamic way.

Of course, doping carries certain meanings within specific contexts. But doping and doping experiences occur in multiple contexts, are undertaken by many types of users, and for a variety of reasons. To capture and describe this variety and mobility in terms of experiences that form doping trajectories, we are introducing the concept of *cumulative recalibration.* We use this concept to describe a process of mobility between cultural contexts and gendered understandings, in which the individual aligns with current cultural goals and ideals in ways that build from and/or may conflict with previous (embodied) experiences, perceptions, or values. Accumulated experiences (understood as part of our sedimented histories) are recalibrated against current contextually-based meanings, values, and goals. This concept helps us to look beyond traditional divides often drawn between sport and fitness or men and women, into contextual and cultural "between(s)" where values, perspectives, and practices may be reformed over time and understood as more or less fluid. Cumulative recalibration thus includes collective/cultural/contextual perceptions as well as individual experiences and histories.

To illustrate this, we will now acquaint the reader with a person we met during fieldwork, a woman named Jessica. We suggest that this portrait can serve as an introduction to the complexity and messiness of individual approaches and decisions to engage in doping practices, a messiness that has seldom been explored in research or public discourse. Jessica's case is not intended to be understood in terms of its particularity, as we will not follow her in detail throughout the book. Rather, Jessica serves to illustrate how cumulative recalibration may manifest as new experiences are gained and practices and ideals are reconceptualized over time. This case illustrates one of many trajectories we will touch on throughout the book, and in other chapters new acquaintances will be made. Following this case study, we will return to the aims of the book and lay out its contents.

Tracing the Doped Body

Jessica is a 37-year-old fitness enthusiast and doping user who describes herself as an active and social person. During her youth and teenage years, she was heavily involved in sports. She played a lot of volleyball and some football. She also tried out gymnastics, basketball, and badminton. Always on the move, picking up her training gear for practice as soon as she came home from school became an automatic routine during adolescence. She continued to play volleyball at a fairly high national level as a young adult, but in her mid-twenties she badly injured her knee. She went through surgery and rehab, training at a gym for a year before she tried to make a comeback to sports. She never succeeded in getting back to her previous physical ability on the volleyball court, as she had simply lost too much time to catch up and her body could not fully throw off the effects of her injury. A few years later, Jessica replaced her involvement in organized competitive sports with the gym and fitness exercise. Initially, she participated in various group fitness activities, but soon she began working out with free weights. She went to the gym almost every day, but she also tried to keep one foot in sport. For a while, she was a second trainer for a group of young girls playing volleyball for her former club.

Jessica was serious and dedicated to her gym training, but she wanted quick results. Living in a big city, she went online and found her way to a forum where people were discussing their results from working with various personal trainers (PTs). She wanted to find a PT who could support her training and diet and help her reach her goals of making her body more fit and muscular. Up to this point, Jessica had not given the idea of using drugs to expedite her training results much thought. On the contrary, this was not something she thought of as a possibility at all at the time. Another two years passed, though, and Jessica still had not found a trainer who she connected with to bring her closer to her fitness goals. She felt that if she was unable to find a PT who was right for her, she needed to take matters into her own hands. This was when she started to rethink her stance on doping. Altering her body and shaping it into her desired form seemed impossible without "help." She discussed the idea with some friends who, like her, had heard about various supplements and substances that could boost progress. Jessica had many questions: Are there any risks? Is it more dangerous for me as a woman? What kind of results can I expect? Living in Sweden, where not only the trafficking of IPEDs is illegal but also possession and use of these drugs, she also wondered how to get hold of IPEDs without risking encounters with the police. Once again, she went online to learn more about doping. Eventually she decided to go for it, but she also decided that she would stop immediately if there were any side effects that she did not expect. Among other things, she was worried that her voice would deepen and her face would change, giving her a more masculine look. She started her first course of substances at the age of 34, filled with both expectation and some fear. Since then she has completed another couple of courses with varied results.

What Jessica's case shows is that perspectives on doping and the doped body can change over time. Things that are more or less unthinkable at one point can become appealing later on or when viewed from another perspective. Central to this narrative is the sense of mobility: Jessica operates in sport and in gym and fitness culture; she also operates in both the online and offline contexts. (Gendered) body ideals and identity claims develop and change over time, as does her approach to potential risks. Jessica carries previous experiences and values with her, updating and modifying her views as her circumstances and ambitions shift or are recalibrated in relation to norms and ideals in the different cultural settings in which she finds herself.

Doping Terminology and Approaches

Approaching and discussing doping unavoidably means becoming involved in a morally charged discourse in one way or another. The choice of terminology is therefore significant in such a social and cultural landscape. One way to talk about doping is to focus only on substances and practices that are prohibited by the World Anti-Doping Agency (WADA). WADA is the global anti-doping policymaking body for much of global sport, responsible for setting international standards across sports and countries. However, WADA's ability to influence anti-doping efforts outside the sphere of organized sports such as in the gym and fitness context is limited. Various National Anti-Doping Agencies (NADOs) under the WADA umbrella simply do not have jurisdiction in the privatized and commercialized gym and fitness context/business, though many elite and amateur sports athletes conduct training in these environments. Another way to approach doping would be to focus on performance enhancing substance use that is prohibited by national law. But this approach is also flawed, as prohibitions outside the sports context vary by country. Thus, whereas some countries have strict laws against these drugs and implement strong measures to reduce the occurrence of IPED use, others do not (Andreasson & Henning, 2019).

Taking this variety of policy limitations into consideration, we have taken a more heuristic approach to doping in this book. When talking about doping, the focus is on practices and understandings from the user perspective. This does not mean we ignore whether certain substances are prohibited in sports or by law *per se*, but we have decentered these parameters in our analysis as these classifications are not our main analytical objective. As an example, it has become increasingly popular in the past few years, especially among some women, to use a substance called 2.4-dinitrophenol (DNP). DNP increases body temperature, making it easier for a person to reduce body fat. However, in many countries such as Sweden (the Swedish Doping Act, 1991:1969), DNP is not prohibited or classified as a doping substance. Rather, it is classed as a toxic substance used for purposes such as wood preservation, dyeing preparations, and making explosives (Personne et al., 2014; Sousa et al., 2020). Users themselves, however, think of and discuss DNP in terms of doping (Sverkersson et al., 2020). Therefore, our focus will be on the users' practices and intentions when using substances (what they understand as doping), rather than on substances by their legal or WADA classifications.

When studying doping outside the context of organized and competitive (elite) sports, researchers have sometimes applied prefixes to highlight contextual distinctiveness. Terms such as "recreational," "exercise," "vanity," and "fitness" have been employed to describe doping within gym and fitness culture (Christiansen, 2009; 2020; Petrocelli et al., 2008; Thualagant, 2012). Here, we have chosen to use the term *fitness doping*. We have two main reasons for this choice. First, it puts the focus on the cultural context of use, as opposed to the specific, organized context of *sports doping*. This contextual binary is one we will aim to collapse in some ways throughout this book, and perhaps even "pair" in terms of bringing the contexts together (see chapter 2). Nevertheless, sometimes we need to specify the contexts in order to bring them down, so to speak. Second, *fitness* anchors the body in the center of the analysis without pinpointing the meanings that lie behind individuals' engagement or disengagement with this practice (Andreasson, 2015). The fitness concept also makes it possible to disrupt a binary often found between social sciences and biomedical perspectives of the physical body. It can describe physical abilities and biomedical conditions of bodies (that can be altered through drug using practices), as well as cultural ideals around self-fulfillment, health, gender, and other factors (Smith Maguire, 2008). Although this book is situated within the social sciences and cultural sociology, we argue for multiple ways of understanding (doped) bodies, the motives and trajectories to fitness doping, doping's gendered dimensions, and potential social and legal responses to the practices and processes of doping. In doing so we also aim, at least partially, to destabilize the prevailing separation between fitness doping and sports doping that academics have contributed to for decades.

Talking about terminology, and with regard to fitness doping in particular, there has also been a tendency among scholars to discuss and approach this in terms of use and abuse. Fueled by media and political discourses, understandings of IPEDs have tended to suggest that using these drugs is "akin to being a gun powder keg about to explode" (Soni & Nasrulla, 2018; see also Gorman, 2017). Evidently, and as part of a pathology paradigm (Moore, 2008), researchers have thus arranged themselves within the dominant narrative of harm. Whereas many studies have tended to discuss doping practices in terms of abuse, recently the term "use" has been put forward. This opens up a discussion on doping as pleasure and for recreational purposes, among other things (Mulrooney et al., 2019). This approach is also more in line with the empirical statements reported in qualitative studies (Andreasson & Johansson, 2020; Christiansen, 2020). Further, the term "abuse" has also been considered morally charged and associated with other drugs (Christiansen et al., 2017). "Abuse" also generally refers to use in ways not normally intended, such as knowingly over-consuming or using substances for purposes or in ways that are likely to increase risk beyond normative use.

Here, we will employ the term *use* when talking about doping. This does not mean that we disregard the research showing that doping may lead to physical and mental health problems, such as increased irritability, depression, cardiovascular disease, liver damage, acne, and hair loss (ACMD, 2010; Pope et al., 2014; Rasmussen et al., 2018). Women run the risk of developing a deeper voice (associated with that of a man), disrupted menstruation, and decreased fertility; gynecomastia, testicular atrophy, and impotence are possible side effects for men (Evans-Brown et al., 2012; Rasmussen et al., 2016). These physical and biomedical effects of the drugs are, of course, also related to users' experiences and how they understand and make meaning of their use practices. This renders them ever-changing in some ways. The occurrence of side effects is also dose-related and linked to users' medical knowledge of and experience with different substances (Monaghan, 2012; Rasmussen et al., 2016).

Aims and Data

In this book we are interested in the increasingly blurry lines between doping-related notions of sports/fitness, masculinity/femininity, online/offline, policy/practice, pleasure/harm, fantasy/lived experience, and healthy/unhealthy lifestyles. Often, such stark categorizations made in public discourse – and by scholars – oppress bodies, which are more dynamic than such labels account for or even allow. By calling these boundaries into question, we are able to recenter the body and its propensity to shift between such categories (cf. Borradori, 2003). We embrace the challenge of going beyond these dichotomies to refocus on doping experiences and meaning-making, particularly how doping contributes to and is impacted by the development of various performance cultures. This will mainly be done through the lens of three thematic arenas forming the overall aim of the book. First, we aim to analyze doping trajectories as they unfold across and between different doping cultures and contexts that have been seen as clearly divided or separated in research and public discourse. Second, as doping (and sport) has been historically understood as a more or less compulsory male preserve, often backgrounding women's experiences and knowledge, we will address women's doping practices and doing gender. Here we will examine the meaning-making and knowledge that is enacted as women users talk about their use, body, and health, both in the context of online communication and away from the keyboard. We will also dissect the ways (hyper)masculinity, sexuality, and the construction of subcultural and sexual spaces are manifest by male users, and the potential harms to relationships and health that this may bring. Finally, we are interested in users' understandings of different responses to doping in terms of prevention and harm reduction, and the consequences these different responses may bring in terms of marginalization and stigmatization. Such responses to doping and users are often formed by national policies and may vary greatly between countries. At the same time, doping responses also need to be understood in relation to international discourses on health, bodies, and risk, among others.

The book mainly uses empirical qualitative data that we have collected jointly and separately over the course of several years. Our fieldwork has primarily been inspired by strategies and concepts developed through ethnographic research, ranging from observations and group discussions to formal interviews and informal talks. Through these, different aspects of IPED users' experiences of doping and its consequences in daily life have been analyzed. Employing a relatively open-ended approach and research design, we have tried to listen and take part in users' lives over an extended period of time in order to capture what is said about doping and how it is practiced. We have also included data from online sources, such as forums in which IPED practices are discussed among peers, using a netnographic approach (a method sometimes described as online ethnography). Further, we also draw on secondary literature on various forms of doping. Data derive from specific countries, including Sweden, the United States, and the United Kingdom, but also include views of online participants from various countries around the world. One benefit of using data from different countries is that it makes it possible to grasp differing perspectives as they evolve in diverse settings, as well as making it possible to distinguish both the common features of doping practices and how national framing concerning prohibition, public discourse, and policy unfold and are met by users based in their geographic location. (For a more thorough discussion of data and methodological approaches, see Appendix and Andreasson & Johansson, 2020; Henning, 2015; Henning & Andreasson, 2019).

Book Outline

In this first chapter we have introduced some of the main arguments we will develop in the rest of the book. We have highlighted some of the existing boundaries between doping in different contexts and related to terminology, as well as responses to doping that are found in both research and public discourse. We also declared our goal of smudging these lines, aiming to deconstruct hegemonic views and narratives built around such distinctions. In *Chapter 2,* we present a general historical background to doping. This is not meant to be a comprehensive and exhaustive history. Rather, we make some historical and thematic stopovers as we examine the ever-changing ways doping has been viewed and understood. In *Chapter 3* the focus is on doping contexts and trajectories, including how users describe their initiation to IPED use. Although we focus on data from fitness dopers, we move between contexts to critically discuss existing typological depictions of doping triggers and trajectories. *Chapter 4* concerns gender and its relationship to doping. Because the male experience is often taken as the default, we initiate this theme with female dopers' narratives, highlighting the changing demography of doping. Here we focus on how women negotiate the meanings of their use in relation to the dominant conceptualizations of this gendered practice, and consider how assumptions around sexuality and femininity are dealt with on a spectrum from women in sports to women in fitness and bodybuilding. We draw on material gathered from an online forum for women and steroids, though not exclusively. In *Chapter 5* we focus on male dopers' ambivalent constructions of masculinity. We address how male users situate their drug use practices in the intersection between marginality and hegemony, and how these men deal with the delicate balance between sexual and other bodily urges, desires, and fantasies on the one hand, and loss of control on the other. *Chapter 6* focuses on responses to the issue of doping, including anti-doping, prevention, and harm reduction. Our discussion will orbit around questions concerning whether anti-doping work connects to public health issues and how it is understood from user perspectives. Finally, in *Chapter 7* we bring these threads together to show that in reconsidering the contextual separations between types of doping, the lines drawn around them begin to melt, transitioning into new ways of understanding trajectories, gender, and response. The book also includes an Appendix where we describe in more detail our methodological considerations and the decisions made when writing this book, alongside a presentation of the data used in the various chapters.

REFERENCES

ACMD. (2010). *Consideration of the anabolic steroids*. Home Office.

Ahmed, S. (2006). *Queer phenomenology. Orientations, objects, others*. Duke University Press.

Andreasson, J. (2015). Reconceptualising the gender of fitness doping: Performing and negotiating masculinity through drug-use practices. *Social Sciences*, *4*(17), 546–562.

Andreasson, J., & Henning, A. (2019). Glocal fitness doping: Policy, practice and prevention in the United States and Sweden. *Performance Enhancement & Health*, *6*(3-4), 103-110.

Andreasson, J., & Johansson, T. (2020). *Fitness doping. Trajectories, gender, bodies and health*. Palgrave Macmillan.

Boepple, L., Ata, R.N., Rum, R., & Thompson, J.K. (2016). Strong is the new skinny: A content analysis of fitspiration websites. *Body Image*, *17*(8), 132–35.

Borradori, G. (2003). *Philosophy in a time of terror. Dialogues with Jürgen Habermas and Jacques Derrida*. The University of Chicago Press.

Christiansen, A. V. (2009). Doping in fitness and strength training environments. Politics, motives and masculinity. In V, Møller., M, McNamme., & P, Dimeo. (Eds.), *Elite sport, doping and public health*. University Press of Southern Denmark.

Christiansen, A. V., Schmidt Vinther, A., & Liokaftos, D. (2017). Outline of a typology of men's use of anabolic androgenic steroids in fitness and strength training environments. *Drugs: Education, Prevention and Policy, 24*(3), 295-305.

Christiansen, A. V. (2020). *Gym culture, identity and performance-enhancing drugs: Tracing a typology of steroid use*. Routledge.

Dimeo, P. (2007). *A history of drug use in sport 1876-1976. Beyond good and evil.* Routledge.

Evans-Brown, M., McVeigh, J., Perkins, C., & Bellis, M. A. (2012). *Human enhancement drugs. The emerging challenges to public health*. North West Public Health Observatory.

Felski, R. (1995). *The gender of modernity*. Harvard University Press.

Gorman, G. (2017). *The deadly crusade to get ripped.* Retrieved from News.com.au. https://www.news.com.au/lifestyle/beauty/for-men/the-deadly-crusade-to-get-ripped/news-story/0457a6e5a0e00ea49980e240fb991579

Henning, A. D. (2015). Health culture and running: Non-elite runners' understandings of doping and supplementation. *Journal of Amateur Sport*, *1*(2), 51.

Henning, A., & Andreasson, J. (2019). "Yay, Another Lady Starting a Log!": Women's Fitness Doping and the Gendered Space of an Online Doping Forum. *Communication & Sport*. https://doi.org/10.1177/2167479519896326.

Klein, A. (1993). *Little big men: Bodybuilding, subculture and gender construction.* State University of New York Press.

Lloyd, S., & Moore, J. (2015). Sedimented histories: Connections, collaborations and co-production in regional history. *History Workshop Journal*, *80*(1), 234-248. https://doi.org/10.1093/hwj/dbv017

Monaghan, L.F. (2012). Accounting for Illicit Steroid Use. Bodybuilders' Justifications. In A, Locks. & N, Richardson (Eds.), *Critical readings in bodybuilding*. Routledge.

Moore, D. (2008). Erasing pleasure from public discourse on illicit drugs: On the creation and reproduction of an absence. *The International Journal of Drug Policy*, *19*(5), 353–358. http://dx.doi.org/10.1016/j.drugpo.2007.07.004

Mulrooney, K. J., van de Ven, K., McVeigh, J., & Collins, R. (2019). Commentary: Steroid madness- has the dark side of anabolic-androgenic steroids (AAS) been over-stated? *Performance Enhancement & Health*. https://doi.org/10.1016/j.peh.2019.03.001

Personne, M., Ekström, M., & Iveroth, M. (2014). 2,4-dinitro-fenol ett dödligt bantningsmedel [2,4-dinitro-fenol a lethal slimming agent]. *Läkartidningen*. 2014;111: CSU7.

Petrocelli, M., Oberweis, T., & Petrocelli, J. (2008). Getting huge, getting ripped: A qualitative exploration of recreational steroid use. *Journal of Drug Issues*, *38*(4), 1187–1206.

Pope, H. G., Kanayama, G., Athey, A., Ryan, E., Hudson, J. I., & Baggish, A. (2014). The lifetime prevalence of anabolic-androgenic steroid use and dependence in Americans: Current best estimates. *The American Journal on Addictions*, *23*(4), 371–377.

Rasmussen, J.J., Schou, M., Madsen, P.L., et al. (2018). Increased blood pressure and aortic stiffness among abusers of anabolic androgenic steroids: Potential effect of suppressed natriuretic peptides in plasma? *Journal of Hypertension*, *36*(2), 277-285.

Rasmussen, J.J., Selmer, C., Østergren, P.B., Pedersen, K.B., Schou, M., Gustafsson, F., Faber, J., Juul, A., & Kistorp, C. (2016). Former abusers of anabolic androgenic steroids exhibit decreased testosterone levels and hypogonadal symptoms years after cessation: A case-control study. *PLoS One, 11*(8): e0161208. Doi: 10.1371/journal.pone.0161208

Smith Maguire, J. (2008). *Fit for consumption. Sociology and the business of fitness*. Routledge.

Soni, A., & Nasrulla, F. (2018). *Be careful of these instant muscle builders. The Tribune*. Retrieved from. https://www.tribuneindia.com/news/trends/be-careful-of-these-instant-muscle-builders/631509.html.

Sousa, D., Carmo, H., Roque Bravo, R., Carvalho, F., de Lourdes Bastos, M., Guedes de Pinho, P., & Dias da Silva, D. (2020). Diet aid or aid to die: An update on 2,4-dinitrophenol (2,4-DNP) use as a weight-loss product. *Archives of Toxicology*. Advance online publication. 10.1007/s00204-020-02675-9.

Sverkersson, E., Andreasson, J., & Johansson, T. (2020). 'Sis science' and fitness doping. Ethnopharmacology, gender and risk. *Social Sciences*, *9*(4), 1-13.

The Swedish Doping Act. (1991:1969). *Dopningslagen*. Stockholm, Sweden: Svensk författningssamling SFS.

Thualagant, N. (2012). The conceptualization of fitness doping and its limitations. *Sport in Society: Cultures, Commerce, Media, Politics*, *15*(3), 409–419.

Waddington, I., & Smith, A. (2009). *An introduction to drugs in sport. Addicted to winning?* Routledge.

Chapter 2

The Interwoven Histories of Sports and Fitness Doping

Just as there are multiple types of doping, there is really no one single history of doping. Even the concept of doping itself is vague and ever-changing. In sports, doping is defined by the World Anti-Doping Agency (WADA) as violating one of eleven anti-doping rules. One of those rules is using any of the proscribed substances on WADA's List of Prohibited Substances. While this might seem straightforward, the Prohibited List is updated annually with new substances added and few removed. Definitions of doping are even less clear outside of organized or WADA-governed sports, such as in spaces like gyms and fitness centers where individuals with a variety of motivations and goals work out. Fitness doping includes using a range of enhancing substances, both legal and illegal. Steroids and other muscle-building substances are included, but so are stimulants, image enhancing drugs (e.g., Melanotan), and weight reducing drugs (e.g., ephedrine). IPED use in these environments also expanded the pool of users beyond bodybuilders to include new populations, including women who are a demographic group still fairly under-researched (Andreasson & Johansson, 2020). The picture widens further if we include cognitive enhancing drugs, also known as "smart drugs," used to increase focus and wakefulness. These are often available only by prescription but can be misused for sports or fitness enhancing purposes (van de Ven et al., 2020). Adding to this, what is considered illicit varies by country.

In this chapter, we examine the cultural history of doping and how it has been understood differently depending on which sport or cultural context is in the limelight. We argue that historians and sociologists have tended to narrow down their focus in effort for specificity – such as aiming to understand doping in cycling or in weightlifting, in Russia, or the former East Germany – and in doing so, some of the more general trends or broad historical patterns related to doping have been backgrounded. Therefore, we show that seemingly disparate histories of doping are, in fact, linked and intertwined with broader cultural and societal trends. On a societal/structural level, the use of doping can, for example, be connected to processes of medicalization (Conrad, 2007) and healthism (Crawford, 2006), which may influence lifestyle choices and understandings of how the body can be legitimately dealt with, enhanced, and changed (no matter which context in focus).

The history presented here will be necessarily schematic and short. Other scholars have published more extensive work on doping developments, though these usually focus on one particular context (see Andreasson & Johansson, 2014; Beamish, 2011; Dimeo, 2007; Gleaves, 2014; Hunt, 2011). Here, we trace how doping in both sports and fitness contexts unfolded in tandem, beginning with early experiments with energy and muscle-building drugs and moving through the decades to the emergent user groups of the commercialized present.

Introducing Amphetamines and Steroids

Much of the earliest sports doping involved various types of stimulants to ward off fatigue brought on by exercise or competition during the late 19th century. Many of these, think cocaine and strychnine, were widely available and unregulated (Courtwright, 2009). The earliest known rule against sports doping dates to the 1908 Olympics and forbade any kind of drug use for the marathon event (Reinold, 2015). Given that there were no tests for stimulants, it is likely marathoners found ways around the rule. Stimulants were also growing in popularity and many drugs were developed during the first half of the 20th century for purposes distinctly unrelated to sports or fitness. For example, amphetamine tablets were introduced to the U.S. market in the late 1930s with approval from the American Medical Association (AMA) (Rasmussen, 2008).

Amphetamines were first available without a prescription, but even after they required a prescription they were so popular that use reached "epidemic" levels during the 1940s and 1950s (Rasmussen, 2008, p.976). Given the widespread use of amphetamines, it is little surprise that athletes would engage as well, especially as there were no rules around their use in sports and they were widely considered innocuous cures for a range of conditions and maladies. Amphetamines gave energy to soldiers during World War II, were used to treat depressive symptoms, and employed as weight loss drugs, while also making their way into sports. Sports restrictions on amphetamines came along with rising fears of health harms related to their wider use, illustrated by the concerns voiced to the AMA about amphetamine use by athletes in 1957 (Rasmussen, 2008). However, sports would not consider amphetamines important or dangerous enough to ban them or begin testing for them until the mid-1960s.

It was around this same time that IPEDs were introduced in bodybuilding. Though experiments with animal testosterone extracts had been carried out since at least the late 1800s, the synthetic anabolic steroids popular today were not available until the mid-20th century. In 1954, an American doctor, John Ziegler, was inspired to produce a synthetic drug based on testosterone after encountering Russian weightlifters using it at that year's World Weightlifting Championships (Kremenik et al., 2006). This drug, called Dianabol, was designed to produce strength gains similar to those resulting from testosterone, but with reduced intensity and a lower number of side effects. It was available for purchase beginning in 1958 and soon became very popular, initially among athletes in the U.S. It was then picked up in the former Soviet Union and other countries around the world. Waddington and Smith (2009) note the Cold War context of Dianabol's emergence:

> Should we not ask whether it is purely coincidental that the two countries which figure centrally in this story – the United States and the Soviet Union – were at the time the world's two superpowers? In this context, it is worth reminding ourselves that the period to which the story relates, namely the 1950s, was the period of the Cold War, in which superpower rivalry war particularly intense, and in which sport was used by each of the superpowers as a means of demonstrating the claimed superiority of its own political and economic system. (p. 52)

The socio-political processes that fueled the development of steroids in a time of conflict between superpowers and international competition were accompanied by other cultural changes. The advent and accessibility of Dianabol also coincided with shifting ideals around male bodies and bodily science (Andreasson & Johansson, 2020). As tastes changed from the Grecian ideals of natural forms in the 1930-40s to the 1950-60's massive, muscular, and defined bodies, Dianabol became a technology of choice in a socio-political landscape of competition between not only superpowers but also superior bodies. It was even suggested within the bodybuilding community that it was the "breakfast of champions." It made its way through not only weightlifting (Rosen, 2008), but into a range of other sports and wider gym and fitness culture. As there were no sports rules or laws against using steroidal products, there was little to prevent athletes and weightlifters from experimenting with them. We can begin to see clear links between experimental use of new forms of synthesized testosterone and stimulants on one hand, and war, sports, modernity, and fitness on the other during the 1940s and 1950s (Yesalis & Bahrke, 2005).

Doping had previously been associated with professional, and thus working-class, sports. The use of drugs for performance had long been considered at odds with amateur values of sports, especially Olympic sport that was based on the notion of the upper-class, gentleman amateur (Christiansen, 2010; Gleaves & Llewellyn, 2014). However, the widespread use of energy and strength improving drugs bled into the worlds of sports and fitness. Without prohibitions or means to detect use, amphetamines and steroids were at least tacitly accepted in sports and society through the middle of the 20th century. This began to change as questions around health and the nature of sports and athleticism were increasingly debated. As concerns about the negative effects of these drugs were raised, the seeds of anti-doping were planted during the late 1950s and would grow into an organized campaign over the following decades (Dimeo, 2007). This new movement would involve sports governing bodies and national governments and impact athletes, bodybuilders, and wider fitness communities.

Anti-Doping, Muscle Mass, and Experimentation

The 1960s-70s were a period of wide social drug use and these permissive attitudes around experimentation were mirrored in sports and gyms. The extensive use of amphetamines and growing use of steroids were both still fairly unregulated by governments, and athletes seemed unbothered by their use. Attitudes towards drug use began to change in the 1970s when fears around recreational and injected drugs, including heroin, led to the declaration of a "war on drugs" in the U.S. Suddenly, attitudes and laws began changing to prohibit the use of recreational drugs. Sports and gym culture were not exempt from these moves, though the two spheres developed in quite distinct but overlapping ways.

Beginning in the mid-1960s, sport began taking the question of doping more seriously than it had previously. The International Olympic Committee (IOC) set up a Medical Commission in 1967 that would chart much of anti-doping's science and testing-based approach up to the present (Henne, 2014). Early sports rules around doping were directly related to what was detectable. Cycling was the site of early tests, mostly as cycling was still recovering from the deaths of Knud Enemark Jensen and Tommy Simpson. Jensen was a Danish cyclist who died while competing in the 1960 Olympics. Though his death was likely due to heat stroke, it was quickly attributed to amphetamine use by the media and anti-doping campaigners (Dimeo, 2007). Indeed, the IOC organized a sub-commission on doping in sport following Jensen's death (Krieger, 2016). Similarly, Tommy Simpson was an English cyclist who died while competing at the 1967 Tour de France. While there were trace amounts of amphetamines found in Simpson's body following his death, there is no evidence that Jensen had abused stimulants. Both deaths were likely brought on by competing in very hot conditions with inadequate hydration, but anti-doping campaigners seized on the doping death narrative to advance their cause (Dimeo, 2007). With a new method of detecting amphetamines in place by 1968, the IOC banned doping and began formal testing at the 1968 Games.

Even though it was fairly widely known by sports officials that athletes were using steroids at this point, the Medical Commission was reluctant to prohibit them without a way of enforcing such a rule. Steroids were not considered to be much of an ethical issue by athletes, but the Medical Commission was opposed on grounds of fairness and beliefs about purity (Dimeo, 2007; Henne, 2014). At this point, steroid use was discouraged but not yet clearly prohibited. A screening test that could determine if steroids were present in a sample was developed by 1974, but further tests would be required to determine which ones (Henne, 2014). The IOC formally placed anabolic steroids on its prohibited list that same year. Pilot testing began at the 1975 Commonwealth Games before beginning full testing at the 1976 Olympics. Though the 1976 tests led to eight disqualifications for steroid use, the tests themselves were quite easy to beat as long as the athlete had stopped using anabolic substances a few weeks before (Hunt, 2011). Despite this, the Medical Commission had proven that it was possible to detect multiple types of doping substances and they were given remit to continue identifying new enhancing substances and developing tests for detection.

As moves to begin addressing the issue of doping in organized sports were picking up steam, a very different atmosphere existed within bodybuilding and gym culture. The 1960s were when the effects of anabolic steroids were becoming highly visible on the bodies of gym-goers (read: bodybuilders), marking the move towards mass and definition as the preferred look (Locks & Richardson, 2012). This was most evident in the world's most recognizable bodybuilder, Arnold Schwarzenegger. He used steroids as part of his training to achieve the standard-setting look of the era, and in doing so he also became a movie star and later also reached the top strata of American politics when elected Governor of California (Andreasson & Johansson, 2020). In his revealing autobiography, *Total Recall: My Unbelievably True-Life Story* (2012), Schwarzenegger (with co-author Petre) also describes how using steroids was openly discussed and seen as a normal part of the bodybuilding scene at the time. Pharmaceutical companies were also developing and distributing effective drugs with fewer side effects in the 1970s, making more products available to athletes looking to enhance their bodies (Verroken, 2006). As more steroids were developed, bodybuilders openly explored new substances and combinations. Bodybuilders were seemingly more than willing to be the guinea pigs of experimental substance use. As in the era of organized sports before anti-doping, there was little reason not to do so: anabolic steroids were legal in most countries and were largely seen as a regular part of the masculine and homosocial aura of gym culture, as well as part of the broader trend of medicalization increasingly taking hold in various aspects of society.

It was also near the end of the 1970s and into the 1980s that women began entering gyms as bodybuilders in their own right (Fair, 1999). Women were not immediately accepted into this (sub)culture, especially on the bodybuilding competition circuit. Still, women bodybuilders at this time continued to gain ground and recognition. Along with taking up weights, women also undertook other training practices that included using muscle-building steroids. These women often faced criticism and abuse as a result of their appearances, thought to be "mannish" or "freakish," and such sensationalist perspectives have been more or less prominent in research since (McGrath & Chananie-Hill, 2009). These bodies gradually began to gain cultural acceptance, and even currency, in the 1980s and 1990s. Similar to the Schwarzenegger effect in men's bodybuilding, celebrities like Linda Hamilton, who starred alongside Schwarzenegger in several of the iconic *Terminator* movies, inspired more women to enter gyms and pick up weights. Hamilton's newly muscular body appeared in the 1989 film *Terminator 2* and fitness media focused heavily on her training for the role, introducing a new era of female muscularity (Baghurst et al., 2014; Brown, 1996). Highly visible female forms with muscle mass and definition – considered mostly masculine traits –helped to begin normalizing women as part of gym and fitness culture. It is probably not a coincidence that this development also coincided with an increased interest in feminist thought and perspectives. During this time, scholars such as Donna Haraway (1988), Judith Butler (1990), Dorothy Smith (1987; 1990), and others fueled the discussion on gender and gender equality. The debate came to focus on the *doing* of gender and, in relation to this, female bodybuilders gained recognition as being *avant garde,* challenging popular and hegemonic notions of gender and stereotypical constructions of muscular masculinities and fragile femininities.

Of course, this does not mean that gym and fitness culture became or has become fully gender equal and able to house equitable opportunities for men and women in their fitness activities. Women's muscle-building practices are often still discussed in terms of a threat to the "natural" gender order, in different ways and to different extents (Washington & Economides, 2016). This becomes abundantly clear in relation to the use of IPEDs, which have continued to be conceptualized in terms of men and masculinity (Christiansen, 2020; Smith and Stewart, 2012), a discussion we will return to at length in chapters 4 and 5. As prohibition picked up support within the sports context in the 1960s-70s, there was a delay in the gym space and subculture. This meant muscle builders could engage in and experiment with various drugs without much question and, apart from the potential health effects from use, with few consequences if they were caught.

Scandals and Spectacles

The 1980s and 1990s were marked by shifting views of IPED use in both sports and fitness contexts. Drug use within bodybuilding was beginning to be questioned as new links were made between fragile masculinity and using steroids to mask these internal insecurities (see Klein, 1993). This painted steroids, and the bodies they built, in an increasingly negative light. This was also tied to drug scandals in sports that brought doping issues to light in a way they had not been previously, and cast IPED-using athletes as morally corrupt. Infamously, Canadian sprinter Ben Johnson's 1988 positive test for steroids highlighted the issue of doping in sports against the backdrop of the sport world's biggest spectacle: the Olympic Games. The controversy following the men's 100-meter track final received a huge amount of media attention and led to government action on steroids and doping. Canada launched an investigation into doping, known as the Dubin Inquiry, that revealed widespread doping across sports in Canada and led to the first independent, national level anti-doping agency (Ritchie & Jackson, 2013). Effects of the Johnson scandal were felt elsewhere. The U.S. was prompted to list steroidal products as Schedule III drugs, making them illegal to possess without a prescription (DEA, 2018; Denham, 1997). Sweden criminalized use and possession of muscle-building drugs in 1991 (Swedish Doping Act, 1991), following a 1989 investigation that showed (fear of) widespread use in and out of sports.

Parallel to these scandals and policy shifts, there was an ongoing fascination with the impact and effects of doping on the body. Unlike in sports where the pageantry of large events was often the centerpiece, the built body became a spectacle unto itself (Liokaftos, 2017). Dedicated international bodybuilders broke competition records for muscle mass, symmetry, and vascularity, at the same time that elite sports athletes continued to break world records. This further fueled the commercialization of bodybuilding by capitalizing on the shock value and allure of these visually imposing bodies, as well as the drug use practices that bodybuilders continually sought to augment their physiques. To a certain extent, the existing prohibitions and harsh judgements of doping could co-exist with a cultural attraction to extreme, commercialized (and potentially doped) bodies (Andreasson & Johansson, 2019). Locks and Richardson (2012) discussed the development of bodybuilding as a subculture in which the archaic entertainment spectacle of the freak show has been creeping back into contemporary popular culture:

> ...bodybuilding publications would start *marketing* other bodybuilders as having "freaky and grotesque muscle groups, including Eddie Robinson (famous for his "guns"– arms), Dorian Yates (famous for his enormous lats – back) / In other words, what was being sold to the "fan" or "consumer" of bodybuilding representations was no longer the pleasure of gazing upon a "perfectible body." (Locks & Richardson, 2012, p.182)

Beginning the late 1980s, professional bodybuilding was sold to the consumer through the representational strategy of "enfreakment." However, this strategy was incompatible with broader cultural trends of fitness and sports. As bodybuilding fed the imagery of "muscle freaks," it was increasingly excluded from the more general fitness trend beginning to take off.

The 1990s were a decade in which both gym/fitness culture and sports underwent significant changes related to commercialization. Fitness as a mass leisure activity expanded as a wave of new fitness franchises catering to a larger market than traditional bodybuilders drew more participants, including new groups of women. This "fitness revolution" (Andreasson & Johansson, 2020) marked the split between health-focused fitness and bodybuilding subcultures that were associated with steroids, narcissism, and generally unhealthy lifestyles (Smith Maguire, 2008). Sassatelli (2011) described this process of cultural separation between fitness and bodybuilding, showing how gym culture and gyms gradually adapted a new cultural guise in which:

> old labels have been replaced in professional texts by neologisms such as "fitness centres" and "fitness clubs". These neologisms have a more luxurious feel attached to them, as well as diverting attention from the competitive, harsh and often very masculine world which was originally associated with the term "gymnasium". (Sassatelli, 2011, p.4)

Following this, and in combination with processes of enfreakment, bodybuilding became increasingly marginalized and separated from the notions of fitness and health(ism). Reports on bodybuilding's dark side (e.g., steroid use, obsessive behaviors, psychological impacts) turned interest away from the sport. Simultaneously, organized sports were undergoing their own shift, as the growing commercialization of international sports pushed through the 1990s. The Olympic

Games began allowing professional athletes to compete, increasing the commercial value of the events throughout the decade. This also raised the profile and visibility of the Games, giving more scope to scrutinizing doping scandals on the Olympic platform.

Fears related to steroid use can also be viewed against the revelations of East Germany's decades-long state doping program. East Germany had been a powerhouse in Olympic sports, earning far more medals relative to its population and economic strength than other countries. Rumors of steroid use by athletes accompanied images of muscular athletes – especially women athletes and the critiques of their overly masculine appearances echoed critiques of women bodybuilders – smashing world records in sports including swimming and athletics (Hunt, 2011). These rumors proved true after details of the extent of the system that included as many as 10,000 athletes emerged in the early 1990s following German reunification (Spitzer, 2006). The East German system was highly regulated by doctors working in tandem with coaches to oversee the athletes' training, diet, and drug consumption.[1] In many ways this highly technical and controlled approach mirrored that of bodybuilders over the same period, coupling a highly routinized lifestyle with steroid use for maximum effectiveness (Klein, 1993). Fears related to the unnatural results of steroid use (Henne, 2014) prompted calls for new drug regulations to address the mess these drugs created.

Clean and Natural: Anti-Doping and Anti-Drug

The natural bodybuilding movement largely coincided with the development of international anti-doping policies in organized sports and deployed many of the same arguments. Natural bodybuilding, done without the use of drugs, emerged in the late 1980s around the time steroids were becoming heavily regulated (Liokaftos, 2019). Similar to the health concerns in sports stemming from Jensen and Simpson's deaths, the IPED-related deaths of prominent bodybuilders in the 1990s, such as Mohammed Benaziza and Andreas Munzer, accelerated the movement towards natural bodybuilding (Liokaftos, 2019). This was also related to the broader health and fitness focus of the fitness revolution and the commercialization of health and healthy bodies. With gyms and fitness moving more into the mainstream during the early 2000s, the doping-fueled bodybuilding subculture of the previous decades was further diminished (Andreasson & Johansson, 2020). These updated ideas of fitness and fitness centers were much more inclusive and commercialized than the previous iterations of (basement) gyms as exclusive masculine and homosocial spaces

[1] The East German system was also highly abusive of its athletes and represents unethical distribution of substances. The system included minority aged athletes and lacked informed consent regarding what drugs were administered and potential side effects. For a more thorough account see *Faust's Gold* by Steven Ungerleider (2013).

(Sassatelli, 2010). The wave of women becoming more engaged with fitness occurred alongside changes in women's bodybuilding, as the sport itself opened up new competition disciplines that encouraged less muscular forms and what were considered to be more traditional and accurate feminine forms (Andreasson & Johansson, 2020). Bolin (2012) described this development at the turn of the century and how disciplines such as Body Fitness, Figure, and, later, Bikini Fitness gained popularity and cultural recognition:

> Like fitness, figure competitions attract women who want to succeed in an industry where beauty and an embodied athletic aesthetic provide career/economic opportunities such as modeling, promoting, endorsing, acting, and other activities related to selling fitness products (i.e., clothing, supplements, weight-loss programs, equipment, etc.). Because figure competition does not require the performance of an increasingly gymnastically oriented routine, it is far less physically demanding than fitness. It does not draw women with the muscular development of bodybuilders. (Bolin, 2012, p. 46)

Traditional ideas of femininity penetrated the competitive and professional levels of women's bodybuilding at this time, pushing it out of the international scene. This was underscored when the International Federation of Bodybuilding and Fitness (IFBB) declared it would strip female bodybuilding from its competitive repertoire. This worked as a way to signal the central stakeholder's intention to clean and "purify" women's engagement in the sport (Douglas, 1966/2003). This move further sanitized women's femininities by adapting to a dualistic and traditional gender order (see McGrath and Chananie-Hill, 2009).

Sports also began a massive clean-up effort in this period. A clear turning point came in 1998 when a range of doping substances were found by French border guards after a car for the Festina cycling team was stopped. French police were in charge of the investigation, which expanded to include several other teams set to compete in that year's Tour de France, though it is likely cycling officials had been at least somewhat aware of the issue given the scale of doping uncovered (Dimeo, 2014). After the Tour debacle, sports organizations were under pressure from national governments and the media to take action (Hunt, 2011). The IOC was the main target of these demands as they were the organization in charge of international anti-doping, but had failed to implement a coherent approach across, and even within, sports (Dimeo, 2014). Following the Festina scandal and other revelations of corruption related to organizing the 2002 Olympics, national governments had lost faith in the organization and demanded more accountability (Hunt, 2011). When the opportunity came for reorganizing anti-doping, national governments pushed for change. The result was WADA, a new public-private hybrid organization founded in 1999 to ensure a single set of policies governed anti-doping across global sport.

WADA and its new commitment to anti-doping would impact perceptions and policies related to substance use across sports and fitness in a variety of ways. Each country was expected to sign onto the WADA Code – the policy setting out global anti-doping rules – and to establish their own national anti-doping agency to enforce the Code. Countries have often had their own local interpretations of what anti-doping is meant to do and what form those efforts should take (Andreasson & Henning, 2019). Some countries have expanded anti-doping to include fitness centers and recreational athletes (Christiansen, 2011), whereas other countries have moved to (at least partially) criminalize doping (e.g., Italy, Sweden, U.S.) through national-level policies (Andreasson & Henning, 2019; Henning & Dimeo, 2018). What these each share is a devotion to the vaguely defined notion of "clean sport," which posits sport is only a right for those athletes who abide anti-doping regulations.

New Users, New Markets

The demographics of IPED use and doping appear to be evolving, as the borders around who engages and why continue to expand. Doping is still commonly associated with bodybuilding and elite sports, especially as high-profile scandals continue to haunt events like the Olympics. The Russia scandal uncovered ahead of the 2016 Summer Olympics revealed the potential size and scope systematic sports doping and corruption could take, despite nearly two decades of organized efforts to stop it (McLaren, 2016). Smaller scandals have further eroded trust in anti-doping, such as the Fancy Bears hack of athletes' anti-doping information and the scandal surrounding Team Sky's use of therapeutic use exemptions (Dimeo & Henning, 2018). Rather than deterring athletes from use as the policies and testing system were intended to do, these scandals have not prevented the spread of doping among recreational sports athletes. Data from several countries indicates that use is occurring among amateur and recreational athletes (cf. FAIR, 2020; Henning & Dimeo, 2015; Seifarth et al., 2019). Anti-doping agencies have also begun targeting recreational athletes in some countries, leading to new groups of athletes becoming entangled in anti-doping (Dimeo & Møller, 2018).

Similarly, fitness doping is adapting to demographic changes (Andreasson & Johansson, 2020). New groups of users, including women and other more routine gym-goers, have opened new markets and new (online) spaces for doping (Bates & McVeigh, 2015; Hanley Santos & Coomber, 2017). These new user groups bring their own motivations and understandings, but also have to negotiate issues such as gender (Henning & Andreasson, 2019). Supply routes for accessing IPEDs are changing, too. This is a result of the combination of new user groups and increased regulations around the sale, possession, and use of IPEDs. While some gyms may still supply their local market, even they face competition from new sellers (Salinas, Floodgate & Ralphs, 2019). Local distributors, on one hand, continue to supply drugs to users and potential users. Van de Ven and Mulrooney (2017, p.13) suggest these "suppliers are often 'over-socialized' into the structure and culture of bodybuilding, and follow the cultural scripts that come with their group affiliation. For these dealers their 'bodybuilding capital' (cultural knowledge, physique, success, etc.) is a form of cultural capital that may be converted into economic capital." On the other hand, there are IPED suppliers who have moved online and become increasingly commercialized, altering both the relationship between buyer and seller and the transmission of expertise around use (cf. van de Ven & Mulrooney, 2017). We can trace a process of globalization through which the doping market is gradually being transformed from one that was socio-culturally embedded to a non-integrated and commercial market, existing in an international and, most often, virtual and anonymous arena (Andreasson & Johansson, 2020, p.39). This displacement and cultural relocation of doping will bring new challenges for users, as well as for national anti-doping policies and law enforcement. We discuss these challenges in chapter 6.

Conclusion

Sports doping and doping in the fitness context have often been considered separately and discussed in terms of having different motivations, trajectories, and results. When we trace the ways athletes and gym-goers have engaged with these substances, as well as how the practice has been understood by policymakers and different stakeholders, the lines between them begin to blur.

For much of the 20th century, sports and fitness doping could be understood as a rational choice for individuals to make. The drugs that many anti-doping policies would be based on – stimulants and steroids – were originally introduced to the public as technologies for improving and enhancing minds, bodies, and lifestyles. There were strong socio-political incentives that served to further boost this development over long periods of time, including the Cold War. Decades of unregulated and widespread use allowed these substances to become socially acceptable as part of medicalization processes and competitions between superpowers that eventually bled into sports and fitness and further drove IPED development. Even after policies prohibited their use, lax testing and enforcement meant many could continue their use largely unabated – at times leading to high levels of celebrity and success for users as the commercial opportunities of sports and bodybuilding spectacles expanded. Consequently, we have an initial phase (parts of which might be recurring in the present) in which the understanding of doping was formed in relation to views about its usefulness, modernity, technological development, and medicalization.

The lines between sports and fitness doping dissolve further when we consider the anti-doping response across sports, and national and global policy developments. Sport prohibitions were often linked with national laws regulating social substance use, including muscle-building drugs favored by bodybuilders (Dimeo, 2007). Indeed, high level sports and gym scandals drove, and still drive, national-level policies around doping substances in many countries. Anti-doping efforts pull new populations (recreational athletes, gym-goers) and arenas (amateur sports, fitness centers) under the anti-doping umbrella, and doping markets are increasingly pushed into new virtual spaces (Fincoeur et al., 2015). This overlaps partly (depending on context) with a historical phase in which anti-doping perspectives and concerns about harm for users and values around clean sport seemed to rule and dominate in public discourse (largely stigmatizing users). There is, however, also a phase in which there is an increased fascination with the spectacular body and how bodily limits could be perforated and put on display in a capitalist and commercial market (Andreasson & Johansson, 2019). In this process it becomes increasingly difficult to separate subcultural doped bodies from the performing body beautiful found in a commercialized market.

Historically, the ways doping has been understood have shifted, moving on a continuum between the subcultural context and broader mainstream developments (Johansson et al., 2017). Although the sport and fitness contexts do not always move in tandem, there is a clear relatedness in approaches and responses. This is exemplified not only through the ways anti-doping has been implemented but perhaps even more clearly in the ways extreme bodies and gender ideals have been pursued, viewed, and met in different times, and how questions concerning health, performance, and cultural recognition manifest. This points to future doping and anti-doping developments potentially becoming even more intertwined than their past, a point we will return to at the end of this book.

REFERENCES

Andreasson, J., & Henning, A. (2019). Glocal fitness doping: Policy, practice and prevention in the United States and Sweden. *Performance Enhancement & Health, 6*(3-4), 103-110.

Andreasson, J., & Johansson, T. (2014). The fitness revolution: Historical transformations in the global gym and fitness culture. *Sport Science Review, 23*(3-4), 91-112.

Andreasson, J., & Johansson, T. (2019). *Extreme sports, extreme bodies. Gender, identities & bodies in motion.* Palgrave Macmillan.

Andreasson, J., & Johansson, T. (2020). *Fitness doping: Trajectories, gender, bodies and health.* Palgrave Macmillan.

Baghurst, T., Parish, A. & Denny, G. (2014). Why women become competitive amateur bodybuilders. *Women in Sport and Physical Activity Journal, 22*(1), 5-9.

Bates, G., & McVeigh, J. (2016). *Image and performance enhancing drugs: 2015 survey results.* Liverpool John Moores University.

Beamish, R. (2011). *Steroids: A new look at performance-enhancing drugs.* ABC-CLIO.

Bolin, A. (2012). Buff bodies and the beast. Emphasized femininity, labor, and power relations among fitness, figure and women bodybuilding competitors 1985-2010. In A. Locks & N. Richardson (Eds.), *Critical readings in bodybuilding.* Routledge.

Brown, J. A. (1996). Gender and the action heroine: Hardbodies and the "point of no return." *Cinema Journal, 3*, 52-71.

Butler, J. (1990). *Gender trouble: Feminism and the subversion of identity.* Routledge.

Christiansen, A. V. (2010). "We are not sportsmen, we are professionals": Professionalism, doping and deviance in elite sport. *International Journal of Sport Management and Marketing, 7*(1-2), 91-103.

Christiansen, A. V. (2011). Bodily violations: Testing citizens training recreationally in gyms. In: M. McNamee & V. Møller (Eds), *Doping and anti-doping in sport: Ethical, legal and social perspectives* (pp 136–141). Routledge.

Christiansen, A. V. (2020). *Gym culture, identity and performance-enhancing drugs: Tracing a typology of steroid use.* Routledge.

Conrad, P. (2007). *The medicalization of society: On the transformation of human conditions into treatable disorders.* Johns Hopkins University Press.

Crawford, R. (2006). Health as a Meaningful Social Practice. *Health 10(2006)*, 401-420.

Courtwright, D. T. (2009). *Forces of habit: Drugs and the making of the modern world.* Harvard University Press.

DEA. (2018). Drug scheduling. Retrieved from https://www.dea.gov/druginfo/ds.shtml

Denham, B. E. (1997). Sports Illustrated, the "war on drugs," and the Anabolic Steroid Control Act of 1990: A study in agenda building and political timing. *Journal of Sport and Social Issues, 21*(3), 260-273.

Dimeo, P. (2007). *A history of drug use in sport 1876-1976. Beyond good and evil.* Routledge.

Dimeo, P. (2014). Why Lance Armstrong? Historical context and key turning points in the 'cleaning up' of professional cycling. *The International Journal of the History of Sport, 31*(8), 951-968.

Dimeo, P., & Henning, A. (2018). The decline of trust in British sport since the London Olympics: Team Sky's fall from grace. In B. Fincoeur, J. Gleaves, & F. Ohl (Eds), *Doping in Cycling: Interdisciplinary Perspectives* (pp. 177-188). Routledge.

Dimeo, P., & Møller, V. (2018). *The anti-doping crisis in sport: Causes, consequences, solutions.* Routledge.

Douglas, M. (1966/2003). *Purity and danger. An analysis of concepts of pollution and taboo.* Routledge.

FAIR (Forum for Anti-Doping in Recreational Sport). (2020). Final report. Europe Active. https://www.ehfa-membership.com/sites/europeactive-euaffairs.eu/files/projects/FAIR/FAIR_Final_Report_web.pdf

Fair, J. D. (1999). *Muscletown USA: Bob Hoffman and the manly culture of York Barbell.* The Pennsylvania State University Press.

Fincoeur, B., Van de Ven, K., & Mulrooney, K. J. (2015). The symbiotic evolution of anti-doping and supply chains of doping substances: How criminal networks may benefit from anti-doping policy. Trends in Organized Crime, 18(3), 229-250.

Gleaves, J. (2014). A global history of doping in sport: Drugs, nationalism and politics. *The International Journal of the History of Sport, 31*(8), 815-819.

Gleaves, J., & Llewellyn, M. (2014). Sport, drugs and amateurism: Tracing the real cultural origins of anti-doping rules in international sport. *The International Journal of the History of Sport, 31*(8), 839-853.

Hanley Santos, G., & Coomber, R. (2017). The risk environment of anabolic–androgenic steroid users in the UK: Examining motivations, practices and accounts of use. *International Journal of Drug Policy, 40*, 35–43.

Haraway, D. (1988). Situated knowledges: The science question in feminism and the privilege of partial perspective. *Feminist Studies, 14*(3), 575-599.

Henne, K. (2014). The emergence of moral technopreneurialism in sport: Techniques in anti-doping regulation, 1966–1976. *The International Journal of the History of Sport, 31*(8), 884-901.

Henning, A., & Andreasson, J. (2019). "Yay, another lady starting a log!" Women's fitness doping and the gendered space of an online doping forum. *Communication & Sport*. Advance online publication. https://doi.org/10.1177/2167479519896326

Henning, A. D., & Dimeo, P. (2015). Questions of fairness and anti-doping in US cycling: The contrasting experiences of professionals and amateurs. *Drugs: Education, Prevention and Policy, 22*(5), 400-409.

Henning, A. D., & Dimeo, P. (2018). The new front in the war on doping: Amateur athletes. *International Journal of Drug Policy, 51*, 128-136.

Hunt, T. M. (2011). *Drug games: The International Olympic Committee and the politics of doping, 1960–2008*. University of Texas Press.

Johansson, T., Andreasson, J. & Mattsson, C. (2017). From subcultures to common culture. Bodybuilders, skinheads and the normalization of the marginal. *SAGE Open, 7*(2), 1-9.

Klein, A. (1993). *Little big men: Bodybuilding, subculture and gender construction*. New York: State University of New York Press.

Kremenik, M., Onodera, S., Nagao, M., Yuzuki, O., & Yonetani, S. (2006). A historical timeline of doping in the Olympics (Part 1 1896-1968). *Kawasaki Journal of Medical Welfare, 12*(1), 19-28.

Krieger, J. (2016). *Dope hunters: The influence of scientists on the global fight against doping in sport, 1967-1992*. Common Ground Publishing.

Liokaftos, D. (2019). Natural bodybuilding: An account of its emergence and development as competition sport. *International Review for the Sociology of Sport, 54*(6), 753-770.

Locks, A., & Richardson, N. (2012). *Critical readings in bodybuilding*. Routledge.

McGrath, S., & Chananie-Hill, R. (2009). 'Big freaky-looking women': Normalizing gender transgression through bodybuilding. *Sociology of Sport Journal, 26*(2), 235–254.

McLaren, R. (2016). Independent investigation report: Part 1. WADA. Retrieved from https://www.wada-ama.org/en/resources/doping-control-process/mclaren-independent-investigation-report-part-i

Rasmussen, N. (2008). America's first amphetamine epidemic 1929–1971: A quantitative and qualitative retrospective with implications for the present. *American Journal of Public Health, 98*(6), 974-985.

Reinold, M. (2015). Drug use in athletics. In V. Møller, I. Waddington & J. Hoberman (Eds), *Routledge handbook of drugs in sport* (pp. 67-77). Routledge.

Ritchie, I., & Jackson, G. (2014). Politics and 'shock': Reactionary anti-doping policy objectives in Canadian and international sport. *International Journal of Sport Policy and Politics, 6*(2), 195-212.

Rosen, D. M. (2008). *A history of performance enhancement in sports from the nineteenth century to today*. Praeger.

Salinas, M., Floodgate, W., & Ralphs, R. (2019). Polydrug use and polydrug markets amongst image and performance enhancing drug users: Implications for harm reduction interventions and drug policy. *International Journal of Drug Policy, 67*, 43–51.

Sassatelli, R. (2010). *Fitness culture: Gyms and the commercialisation of discipline and fun*. Palgrave Macmillan.

Schwarzenegger, A., & Petre, P. (2012). *Total recall: My unbelievably true-life story*. Simon & Schuster.

Seifarth, S., Dietz, P., Disch, A. C., Engelhardt, M., & Zwingenberger, S. (2019). Seifarth, S., Dietz, P., Disch, A. C., Engelhardt, M., & Zwingenberger, S. (2019). The prevalence of legal performance-enhancing substance use and potential cognitive and or physical doping in German recreational triathletes, assessed via the randomised response technique. *Sports, 7*(12), 241.

Smith, A. C. T., & Stewart, B. (2012). Body perceptions and health behaviors in an online bodybuilding community. *Qualitative Health Research, 22*(7), 971–985.

Smith, D. (1987). *The everyday world as problematic. A feminist sociology*. Northeastern University Press.

Smith, D. (1990). *The conceptual practices of power. A feminist sociology of knowledge*. Northeastern University Press.

Smith Maguire, J. (2008). *Fit for consumption: Sociology and the business of fitness*. Routledge.

Spitzer, G. (2006). Sport and the systematic infliction of pain: A case study of state-sponsored mandatory doping inn East Germany. In Loland, S., Skirstad, B. and Waddington, I. (Eds), *Pain and Injury in Sport: Social and Ethical Analysis* (pp. 109-126). Routledge.

The Swedish Doping Act. (1991:1969). Dopningslagen. Svensk författningssamling SFS.

Ungerleider, S. (2013). *Faust´s gold. Inside the East German doping machine*. St. Martin´s Publishing Group.

Van de Ven, K., & Mulrooney, K. (2017). Social suppliers: Exploring the cultural contours of the performance and image enhancing drug (PIED) market among bodybuilders in the Netherlands and Belgium. *International Journal of Drug Policy, 40*, 6–15.

Van de Ven, K., Mulrooney, K., & McVeigh, J. (Eds). (2020). *Human Enhancement Drugs*. Routledge.

Verroken, M. (2006). Drug use and abuse in sport. In D. R. Mottram (Ed.), *Drugs in sport* (4th ed., pp. 29–63). Routledge.

Waddington, I., & Smith, A. (2009). *An introduction to drugs in sport. Addicted to winning?* Routledge.

Washington, M. S., & Economides, M. (2016). "Strong is the new sexy: Women, CrossFit, and the postfeminist ideal." *Journal of Sport and Social Issues, 40*(2): 143–161. doi:10.1177/0193723515615181.

Yesalis, C. E., & Bahrke, M.S. (2005). Anabolic steroid and stimulant use in North American sport between 1850 and 1980. *Sport in History, 25*(3), 434-451.

Chapter 3

Trajectories, Cultural Recalibration, and Contextual Mobility

Like many forms of illicit behavior, the prevalence of doping in sports and fitness contexts is unclear. Though WADA's annual rate of positive sports doping tests remains fairly consistent at 1-2%, researchers have put the likely prevalence much higher, at rates between 14-57% (de Hon, Kuipers & van Bottenberg, 2015; Elbe & Pitsch, 2018; Ulrich et al., 2018). Prevalence of fitness doping is also unclear, though the extent of use seemingly varies greatly between countries. For example, one study estimated that in Cyprus as many as 11.6% of young people in gyms, mainly men, used IPEDs (Kartakoullis et al., 2008), whereas these numbers have been estimated to be 4-6% in countries such as Sweden and the U.S. (Johnston et al., 2018; Pope et al., 2014; Swedish National Institute of Public Health, 2011).

Statistics and prevalence work can be useful for understanding the scale of doping, but they are unable to capture significant, non-quantifiable differences, such as those related to national contexts, sports, and culture. As such, various stakeholders such as policymakers, representatives from organizations such as WADA and the International Health, Racquet and Sportsclub Association (IHRSA, the trade association for the health and fitness club industry), doping researchers, and journalists have made efforts to paint a global picture of the current doping situation. Often these pictures are really only snapshots and are, at best, coarse, providing limited information about the people and experiences behind the numbers. They also tend to produce impressions of doping as being a contextually immobile phenomenon. As noted in the previous chapters, the separation between sports and fitness has tended to emphasize particularities and differences, and in doing so also ignored and "zoomed out" from the possible interconnections and similarities in doping routes and trajectories. One could go even further and conclude that different performance cultures such as cycling, wrestling, weightlifting, and bodybuilding, to mention a few, have been treated more or less unevenly. Most discussions have favored a focus on numbers of users rather than comparing experiences or considering potential subcultural overlaps.

This chapter addresses some of the blind spots in the research related to trajectories and motivations for fitness and sports doping. Similarly to how the histories of doping discussed in chapter 2 have been considered separately, previous research has sometimes assumed that doping triggers are bound by single contexts. As a result, factors such as supply access, local or online knowledge, peer support, local policy context, and ongoing use or cessation based on desired effects and results have sometimes been left out of the equation. Arguably, various doping typologies effectively drop in at the point of use without consideration of all the processes that actually allow use to start, continue, and/or stop (a discussion we will return to in the following chapters).

In the next section, we present a background to, and point of departure for, looking at doping trajectories. This is followed by a short section in which we present some central concepts that we use in this chapter to disrupt the ideal-type models of sports and fitness doping users and motivations. Then, we move onto a more comprehensive case study of one doping user. We will look at how this person was shaped by sports experiences and how these were later paired with gym and fitness exercises. We follow this person over the course of several years to show how his doping trajectory was not so much a linear process, but rather the result of a turbulent and, in some ways, unpredictable route and series of lifestyle choices. From there we shift online, exploring the ways users of an online doping forum describe the winding, and sometimes context-crossing, paths they took to IPED use. Here we also interrogate the ways users must navigate values, experiences, and practices across and between contexts through a process of *cumulative recalibration.* This chapter builds on data gathered through ethnographic fieldwork, using a case study-based approach that focuses on a person with longtime experience of both using IPEDs and coaching others in their use. Importantly, this person has operated in the sports and fitness contexts simultaneously. The online material we use in the chapter was gathered from an online platform called *ThinkSteroids,* consisting of a plethora of different forums where users can discuss IPEDs and exchange experiences (see Appendix for further information on methodology and method).

Typologies as Heuristic Tools and their Limitations

To understand doping trajectories and motives it is vital to consider how users themselves view this practice, and how it gradually takes form within daily life relative to thoughts about the body, performance, beauty, friendships, risks, and more. Several studies have sought to capture doping motivations and trajectories. Sports scholars have traditionally debated sports doping in terms of an addiction to winning, while use in the gym context has been primarily connected to young men and their efforts to construct a masculine body and identity (Lucidi, 2008; Sagoe et al., 2014). Such (often) structural-functionalist perspectives of use, usually based on quantitative measures and regression analyses, have been prominent, especially when this research field was initiated in the 1990s (Brennan et al., 2017).

More recently, new models and typologies that depict users and use types have been developed. For example, Christiansen et al. (2017) offer a theoretically-informed typology of fitness dopers as a heuristic tool to expand our understanding of doping motives. Instead of simply considering young men with concerns about muscles as a homogenous group, they present four different ideal types of male users: The Expert type, the Well-being type, the YOLO type, and the Athlete type. As the different labels suggest, individuals approach doping differently and with distinct motives for their use. For the Expert type, doping is more or less an applied science project. This type is fascinated by the effects of the drugs and how pharmaceuticals can be optimized in order change the body in a desired direction. In a way, this is the doping "nerd" who reads medical papers and tries to find the perfect formula of substances, diet, and training to achieve optimal results and the ideal body. The Well-being type is not as risk or result oriented, but instead engages in doping in order to feel good about himself. Then there is the YOLO type, who embraces risk behaviors in the pursuit of excitement and new experiences. You want to live life fully since "you only live once" would be a motto for this type. Finally, we have the Athlete type, whose primary reason for engaging in doping is to perform competitively, usually in bodybuilding or a similar discipline. This typology offers a variety of doping motives, but it was based on male users and their narratives. As such, it does not include women's doping experiences, despite women being a potentially growing demographic group engaging in doping practices (Andreasson & Johansson, 2020). Though this typology can give us significant insights and coarse tools to understand doping motives, there are limitations to such models in terms of being able to capture processes and socio-spatial changes. This becomes evident when closing in on the concepts and complex processes of identity construction as a relational and ever-changing enterprise, for example. Typologies are by nature more or less static and immobile, whereas identities, lifestyles, and cultures are not.

At the same time, the Athlete type can be connected to how use is understood in the elite sports context and the great efforts elite athletes have made to win at any cost. Doping behaviors of the highest-level athletes have mainly been discussed in relation to athletes' eagerness for increased performance and motives connected to competition, prizes, records, and fame (Bloodworth & McNamee, 2010; Christiansen, 2010; Outram & Stewart, 2015). Mirroring the goals of Christiansen et al. (2017) to classify types of fitness doping, Henning and Dimeo (2014) examined doping cases in U.S. cycling. They found a diversity of cases that expand on a simplistic, one-dimensional understanding of doping as risky and cheating. Contrary to this belief about sports doping, they established a typology that challenges the one-size-fits-all approach to anti-doping. They suggest that anti-doping work has been targeted at and built around elite professionals and then applied to all, resulting in the neglect of various types of use behaviors and motivations among (elite and amateur) athletes. They call for a need to rethink current approaches to how sports doping is understood and addressed, especially at lower competitive levels. Though this typology moved beyond the elite/amateur sports divide and problematized the idea of doping intent, it was based only on known doping cases in cycling in one country. This potentially missed out on alternative motivations and circumstances and could not account for the various routes by which athletes come to engage in doping.

Trajectories and Contextual Mobility

In order to capture some of the complexities involved in doping trajectories, we take a cultural sociological approach in this chapter. Doping is discussed as a practice that gradually takes form, becoming a possibility over time and in relation to social contacts and cultural contexts. Thus, we understand "trajectory" as interwoven with identity and processes of becoming acquainted with a particular practice and context. This perspective is exemplified in Becker's (1953) now classical study of marijuana users. He explained that drug use:

> /…/ is the result of a sequence of social experiences during which the person acquires a conception of the meaning of the behavior, and perceptions and judgments of objects and situations, all of which make the activity possible and desirable. Thus, the motivation or disposition to engage in the activity is built up in the course of learning to engage in it and does not antedate this learning process. (Becker, 1953, p. 235)

Following Becker, we look at some of the processes through which use becomes possible/reasonable. An individual's doping trajectory can, for example, start with early experiences in youth sports and/or in physical education in school. Later in adolescence these experiences are complemented with experiences from gym and fitness workouts and perceptions of bodily capabilities, limitations, and doping in this context. We suggest that initial understandings linger in bodies as well as individuals' understandings of doping; individuals have their own sedimented histories (Ahmed, 2006).

However, emphasizing the possibility for contextual mobility and individual agency, these processes are not to be understood as piled up, but rather as reflexive and cumulative. Like the way the image in a kaleidoscope changes when it is moved, peoples' perspectives change as they move through time and between contexts. As individuals are rarely contextually bound, and doping experiences occur in multiple contexts with diverse cultural conceptualizations of such practices, we suggest that acquired experiences and understandings of doping are continuously recalibrated and negotiated. As noted in the introductory chapter, this perspective opens up the concept of (contextual/cultural) *cumulative recalibration*, which can be used to describe how the individual aligns with (or relates to) current cultural goals and ideals in ways that build from and/or may conflict with previous (embodied) experiences, perceptions, or values. This discussion and these theoretical tools will be used here to describe and analyze the processes of becoming a doping user, but will also echo in the chapters that follow. Now we zoom in and meet one of the users who, through repeated interviews, has contributed a narrative on his doping trajectory.

Between Sports and Fitness Doping

Yared, who works in IT and media, is in his late 30s and currently lives in Stockholm with his girlfriend. Before moving to the city, he lived in a smaller village on the east coast of Sweden with his parents and younger brother. Besides school, he usually hung out with friends and played sports as a teenager. He particularly enjoyed wrestling, which he was "pretty decent in." He also tried football for a while during his teens but it was not his favorite, so he dropped out of football after a few years to focus on being a junior wrestler:

> I started out as a wrestler, and was on a fairly advanced level, as a junior wrestler. Then I wanted to improve my performance during one summer. You know, like a summer camp thing. So, I got into this thing, I got into lifting the weights. Actually, it was my uncle, he took me to a gym. He thought that I needed to put on some muscles and weight. For the wrestling. And I did. I did the weights that summer. It was only the summer. But I got to know some people there. I was young and it was like during a time when I needed my parents' permission to train, I remember. I needed it to even be allowed to be at the gym. But, I kept on going, to that gym. And it was still the same people there. Then in upper secondary school I kept on a bit, but the focus on wrestling decreased. I lost interest a bit.

Yared was devoted to his training routine for several years during his adolescence in order to become a competitive wrestler. Like many teenagers, he trained a couple of days per week and occasionally competed on the weekends. Usually, his mother or father would drive him and some wrestling friends to competitions. His parents were supportive of his interest in wrestling and his physically active lifestyle. After graduating and beginning work, the strict schedule required to train with a group of wrestlers on specific days and times every week made it challenging to keep up his routine. He turned to the gym instead and began a fitness program. Yared's move is not uncommon, as many young athletes later replace their involvement in organized sports with training in the gym. Working out in the gym is often less structured in terms of time and duration, making it more flexible to fit in around other commitments and responsibilities.

After a few years as an "average gym-goer," Yared felt his training had plateaued and decided that he needed to do something new if he wanted to see new results. At the time, he was not overly familiar with doping but had discussed it a bit with some friends and had some ideas about where to get support for starting a course of IPEDs. He was pretty ignorant about the first substances he bought, but he trusted the person who sold them and who gave him advice about how to structure his course. This initial course of steroids was followed by many others. Yared described how he became interested in steroids not only for their visible results, but because he wanted to learn about the substances themselves. He wanted to understand what they did "on a molecular level" within the body. He also did some subcultural research on IPEDs and invested quite a bit of time and energy in reading about substances, their intended effects, possible side effects, and various other aspects on an American online forum. For a short while he also decided that he wanted to know and feel the effects of different substances – an embodied, physical experience – so he made it his goal to try out as many steroids as possible. Perhaps unsurprisingly, this risky pursuit did not go completely as planned.

> I am someone who has got a real thirst for knowledge. I want to learn about everything. And I have pretty much tried everything on myself over the years, for good and for bad. But due to this I have learned what works and why. I also know why something doesn't work. Many people just go about and do their course, but I always have an idea behind my courses. There is an idea behind everything. I have these written notebooks, quite a few actually. I have gathered a lot of data over the years writing and analyzing my courses and results. (…) Then, of course there have been times when I have gotten into it too much. One time for example, I got these cramps because I was lacking fluids and that thing ended up in a couple of days in hospital and me nearly dying.

Following his health problems related to his excessive and sometimes careless use, Yared realized he needed to change his approach to steroids. His heavy use increasingly stressed his body, but he could also see that he had become quite proficient with steroids thanks to his ethnopharmacological stock of knowledge built from his experiments over the years. This was the type of knowledge requested by competitive bodybuilders and others interested in fitness. Before long, he became a coach and included giving advice and planning steroid courses as part of his service.

> I am a so-called grey zone coach. After all, I make all kinds of schedules because I am so informed on the medical side too. I tend to direct my schedules and the schemes that I make like that, including this. Maybe this is why I am so popular. I can do schemes for the diet, for their exercise regimes and combine this with chemistry so to speak. And it is very much, what to call it, yeah, that's a grey zone. And this is something I struggle with everyday. What if someone asks for advice, being coached, he pays me and then comes the question on doping. And I feel like, it's difficult, cause it is still illegal (…) what if they misuse my knowledge and does something stupid.

Though he mainly operated within the fitness industry at the time, Yared gradually became a well-known name in subcultural doping circuits. He was regarded as "an expert" on steroids and soon other types of athletes started to approach him. He trained bodybuilders but he also met elite athletes who wanted advice on how boost their performance. His coaching "grey zone" seemingly fell into the space between sports and fitness. Contrary to prevailing public opinion and views about fair play, he saw a different reality from what most encounter or think of when they watch, in this case, Swedish elite athletes.

> I have sold steroids for many years. And I have sold to some top athletes in Sweden as well. I was a so-called reliable source. Someone they knew that they could buy from with discretion. You know they could buy it from me and the word wouldn't get around. You see? There were quite a few top athletes actually. And you know average Joe will doubt this, saying these guys are clean athletes, they are the good guys. If they only knew. I remember Ludmila Engquist (Swedish citizen originally from Russia who competed in 100 meter hurdles and bobsleigh). She was great and when she won she said, "I love Sweden and Sweden loves me," and I knew already then what she was up to. But the public didn't know. Even the Swedish king clapped his hands. Then she got caught, and everybody turned their backs on her. She came from Russia and all that, they said, instead of realizing that this is part of sports. You can see it even in soccer, there is use of different sorts, stretching from steroids to different medications for asthma, etc. But, still, there is a search for this cutting edge.

As he moved up in the "franchise" of supplying doping substances, Yared became a serious actor in both the sports and fitness contexts. He built up quite a bit of social and cultural capital and was considered a reliable source, a status earned through his successful trafficking activities and coaching business.

Today, Yared is not heavily involved in the trafficking side of things. He still uses occasionally and he sometimes "helps out" if others seek out his advice or network. Working in an office setting he also sees how views of IPEDs are gradually changing. When he started working in his current job, he felt that his lifestyle and voluminous body were questioned and seen by his colleagues as too big or somehow unacceptable. Over time he came to be viewed as somewhat inspirational.

> It wasn't accepted at all when I started to work here. But now, it´s been three years and I have kind off educated them gradually. Because I cannot hide who I am forever and what I like and what kind of sports I do. But it all started with the fact that everybody I worked with were these couch-potatoes, like nice offices, big bosses, high up in the hierarchy, and ended up with my closest boss who used to weigh 160 kilograms now weighs in on some 95 kilos. He has trained and dieted himself down to this level. And he, I work for a news magazine at the moment, and he tells me that he has completely changed his mind about how things are.

Yared was able to change his boss's mind about using steroids, to the point that he aided him in using a "moderate level" course. This is potentially surprising given Swedish intolerance to doping (see chapter 6). Both trafficking and use of steroids is illegal in Sweden and are largely understood as a social problem. Steroid use has been connected with all sorts of negative cultural attributes, including violence and unhealthy lifestyles (Andreasson & Henning, 2019). Fitness doping is regarded in much the same way as recreational or addictive drug use, as a destructive practice to be prevented and policed. Despite this, a fitness doping subculture exists within Sweden, as in other countries. Evidence of this can be found in online forums where users can anonymously discuss their use and challenge national policies and general views on IPEDs (Andreasson & Johansson, 2016). Online communities work to make doping an acceptable subcultural practice, though changing broader cultural views is much more difficult. Being able to calibrate his experiences and knowledge of doping from different contexts (e.g., sports, fitness, national intolerance) Yared was, however, able to align and combine perspectives in a way that is formative not only for his own doping trajectory but also serves as an important ingredient in the formation of others' trajectories. Yared's case shows how the formation of his trajectory seems to take place in what can be described as the interfaces between sport/fitness, subculture/mainstream, and online/offline (cf. Bhaba, 1994). It is clear that Yared's previous experiences, the processes of getting acquainted with doping practices through "IPED schooling," and how the practice is understood in different contexts – his mobility – are central ingredients in how he has learned to navigate the cultural landscape and doing of doping. As suggested in this case, there might be several sources of inspiration in the process of IPED schooling. One possible source is found in the context of online communication, including how dopers approach doping in different forums. We discuss this in the next section.

Online Communities and Legitimization

Online communities for people using or interested in using IPEDs have become an important source of knowledge sharing, support, and discussing experiences (Andreasson & Johansson, 2016). The public communication between members on a forum enables us to trace members' experiences of becoming dopers, often moving from organized sports into gym and fitness in ways similar to Yared. This type of movement reflects the cultural relocation of physical activities, clearly visible in the expansion of the global and commercialized fitness industry in the past two decades among youth and young adults. Online records also allow us to look at how sports practices and ideals around performance and bodily capabilities are potentially reinterpreted or translated when brought into the fitness context. Along with this, values and beliefs related to doping must be recalibrated as members move between subcultural contexts.

One popular platform consisting of an array of thematized forums for discussing different aspects of IPED use is *ThinkSteroids.com.* This platform provides a variety of discussion threads for its global membership to discuss a range of steroid related topics. One key forum on *ThinkSteroids* is called "New Member Introduction" (NMI), where we turn our attention in this section. Focusing on how new members approach doping and ask questions about use in the context of online communication can give insights into their doping trajectories as they unfold. The data here have been analyzed using a netnographic methodology (see Appendix).

Though anyone can read the threads on *Thinksteroids* forums without an account, once someone wants to post or respond to posts they must create an account, with many using pseudonyms for anonymity. The NMI forum contains introductory posts from new members, often used as a way to state one's motivations, current levels of fitness, goals, and previous or future plans for steroid use. New members often used these posts as a way of legitimizing themselves – demonstrating their competence by sharing experiences with physical activities and/or doping. Usually when presenting themselves, new members also showed a certain level of ethnopharmacological knowledge in their use with a variety of abbreviations for substances they have used, which are unlikely to be understood by uninformed potential users. In this way, new members can signal their acquaintance with certain subcultural values and doping practices when engaging in discussions. For increased readability, however, we have tried to explain the abbreviations used where deemed necessary.

> Been on a guest on the board on and off for about a year. Just registering now, mainly into powerlifting. Best total 1840lbs in knee wraps at 267lbs, trying to reach international elite status at 275. Basically just ran testosterone the last year and some Dianabol last prep [before the last competition], looking to learn what I can and hopefully keep up with a log in the powerlifting forum. I'm still a rookie to powerlifting really and anabolics but I'd love to help where I can as well. (DbolBob)

By indicating his competitive powerlifting level and history, DbolBob showed his knowledge of both lifting and steroid use. Listing his weight and combined powerlifting weight flags to others how accomplished he is already, despite referring to himself as a rookie. This and his offer to help others afforded him a level of social and bodily capital on the forum that works to legitimize him and his voice within the community. Other new users may rely on previous sports experience as a way of legitimizing themselves.

> What's up fellas. Football guy here. Played through college and had a cup of coffee in the pros. I am 31yrs old. Currently 5'10 177lbs.
>
> I still do a lot of speed training on top of weights as that's what I am used to doing. I've been on growth hormones for a few months now and really starting to see the benefits come out. Running furious daily. (WalterCampOnhGH)

Similarly, to DbolBob, WalterCampOnhGH listed his sports achievements as a way of indicating his experience and skill. Noting that he played American football at the collegiate and professional levels signals that he has deep experience in training and higher than average sporting achievements. This transfer of capital from sports to fitness highlights how closely linked these contexts are, and that these experiences are mutually understood as important and credible currency across contexts and physical cultures.

The online context allows people to meet anonymously, including those who may be outside an individual's normal social circles. This can result in moving between contexts, as athletes often engaged in the forums to gain new expertise once they have left their sports careers – or to learn to support their current sports career through steroid use.

> I'm 39yrs old, 6'2, 190LBS, body fat 12%. I've been lifting off and on for the last 16 years or so. Endurance training, combat sports, and bodybuilding. I'm too old for all but the latter and am now focused on physique since my body is aging and I cannot bust my ass for 4 hours a day of intense training. I currently have a good bodybuilding training protocol in place and my diet is straight. Got back in the gym 1 1/2 years ago after a Rotator Cuff/Labrum repair. I've been on TRT [testosterone replacement therapy] since September of 2018 and have gotten dialed into my lab numbers. The last 3-4 months I've played around with my prescribed 200mgs T-Cyp [Testosterone cypionate] weekly dose since I only need 140mgs to stay in the normal ranges for T, E2, CBC, Lipid numbers, [Testosterone, estradiol, complete blood count, complete cholesterol test] etc... (RoidRepair)

Much like Yared's case and WalterCampOnhGH's introduction, many of the forum members situated their current fitness interests in their sporting pasts. Members described moving fluidly from organized sports to fitness as a normal progression of interest. RoidRepair even described the simultaneity of such pursuits, as engaging in sports did not exclude engaging in fitness and vice versa. Doping seems to sit in between these two contexts. Instead of approaching sports and fitness doping in terms of difference and diverse motives and rationales, we see here how doping seemingly bridges contextual separations often made by scholars and in public discourse.

Indeed, some users described a more circular trajectory that wound around fitness and sports contexts and included starting and stopping use based on current goals or health status.

> I did my first 12-week cycle of Test and Deca [Deca-Durabolin, brand name for Nandrolone] when I was 22yo. I spent 2yrs researching before converting to the dark side. I used to contribute to the Steroid World website back between 2001-2003. At the time, it was a vault of info. I then followed up that cycle with a Test and Eq [Equipoise, brand name for Boldenone

> Undecylenate] cycle, which would be my last (...) My interests changed and with the weight off, feeling lighter and better, I took up running and cycling. I then added swimming in and completed a few triathlons, marathons and other road races. I discovered I was particularly good at cycling and focused on this as my primary sport up to today. During the past 18years, I have not even though of using AAS. However, as I approach 40yo, I've been giving overall health another focus. I recently had a cardio/inflammation/blood panel completed all good. I also just had a T test done at the urging of a few peers no results back yet. The possibility of low T triggered my interest in AAS again. (DrVader)

DrVader's description of his trajectory from fitness to sports and back to fitness was accompanied by a contextually informed change in doping views and practices. Once he moved from the fitness context into sports, the notion of continuing or importing his doping habits was culturally recalibrated, becoming unthinkable. Doping was something for the gym and not for competitive sports, despite a clear willingness to engage in doping and understanding the benefits it could bring. This may be linked to wider, morally-laden social views of sports doping. DrVader also delineated health as a separate issue from either fitness or sports, relating it instead to medical tests and overall health. Divorcing health from sports and fitness is notable, as it suggests his engagement with both was based on a very different set of motivations. This change ultimately led him back to considering steroids, suggesting that doping can be understood as compatible with overall health. Thus, sports and fitness doping are embedded within their respective cultural localities and connected to broader trends of medicalization and neoliberal values of individual choice linked to healthism (Conrad, 2007; Crawford, 2006).

There is also evidence that residual values of "clean sport" and "fair play" from the sports context remain in the fitness context. In one thread, a member asked for a recommendation for substances to gain an edge in competition. Though what type of competition was not specified (speed, strength, and endurance were all included in the question), one reply focused more on the stated desire to enhance sports performance.

> Just curious why you feel you would need drugs to maintain weight and sustain speed strength and endurance? Or what you really meant was. What drugs can I take to cheat in my sport so I can have an unnatural advantage over all the natural athletes? Two different answers IMO. (NattyNo)

This type of response to a post in a steroid forum is striking. This forum is a place where all types of steroid use for any number of purposes or goals are openly discussed, supported, and normalized. However, by relating use back to wanting to improve in the sports context, the post was read as the poster wanting to cheat. NattyNo was at least interested in using steroids themself, if not actually using them, but still points to the natural/unnatural divide that has underpinned anti-doping in sport (equivalent to that of open bodybuilding vs. natural bodybuilding in the fitness context). This suggests that even as individuals and bodies may slide between contexts, values from one may linger on and need to be recalibrated in the other. These kinds of "hangover values" are then dealt with in a variety of ways as individuals renegotiate the meaning of doping and navigate the prevailing subcultural views of the practice. At times these reinterpretations can appear disjointed or even contradictory.

Conclusion

Through the cases of Yared and the members of the *ThinkSteroids* online community, we have shown the difficulty of drawing clear lines between the sports and fitness contexts when it comes to doping practices, values, and beliefs. As bodies are unfixed and changeable across and even within these contexts, so are views, behaviors, and, thus, doping trajectories. The bodies represented in the data in this chapter operate in a space of in-betweenness: between sports and fitness; online and offline; subculture and mainstream. Yared, for example, was able to shift some perceptions around fitness and doping, despite prevailing negative cultural views of the practices. This made the practice available as a possibility for more than the bodybuilders who he initiated his career with as a coach. There are also contextual overlaps and connections between groups. Expertise and experience in one context can intersect with and work to legitimize individuals in another, as in the NMI forum introductory posts. Many drew on sports experience or backgrounds using IPEDs at an earlier stage as evidence of social and symbolic capital and to position themselves within the community. In this way, experiences and knowledge are accumulated and practices and views are recalibrated when the individual moves between different contexts, cultures, and settings.

Trajectories to doping in any context are rarely linear or linked to a single motivation or decision, or even a clear combination of knowable triggers. Drawing on typologies of fitness and sports doping can be useful for understanding broad motives or general dispositions, but these are not meant to provide detail or insight into the lived experiences that lead to doping as a legitimized practice. Although this chapter builds from, and is limited to, a single case study and communication gathered from an online forum, it illustrates how doping trajectories often are winding or even circular. Trajectories to doping develop gradually, and with much reconsideration of individual-level goals and broader cultural/structural constraints and freedoms, as each individual progresses towards doping. The views that doping is for the young man looking to build a masculine body or the athlete determined to win at all costs are, in that sense, somewhat outdated and reflective of a static view, a snapshot, of who comprises sports and fitness communities. Indeed, individuals may move from sports to fitness, fitness to sports, or engage in both simultaneously – all but dispelling the notions of a single route to doping, a single type of doper, or of doping as a contextually-specific process. This will become even clearer – or perhaps more complex – when we move to consider gender and doping and then again when we consider the impact of local policies.

REFERENCES

Ahmed, S. (2006). *Queer phenomenology. Orientations, objects, others.* Duke University Press.

Andreasson, J. & Henning, A. (2019). Glocal fitness doping: Policy, practice and prevention in the United States and Sweden. *Performance Enhancement & Health, 6*(3-4), 103-110.

Andreasson, J., & Johansson, T. (2016). Online doping: The new self-help culture of ethnopharmacology. *Sport in Society: Cultures, Commerce, Media, Politics, 19*(7), 957–972.

Andreasson, J., & Johansson, T. (2020). *Fitness doping. Trajectories, gender, bodies and health.* Palgrave Macmillan.

Becker, H. S. (1953). Becoming a marihuana user. *American Journal of Sociology, 59*(3), 235–242.

Bhaba, H. (1994). *The location of culture.* Routledge.

Brennan, R., Wells, J.S.G., & van Hout, M.C. (2017). The injecting use of image and performance-enhancing drugs (IPED) in the general population: a systematic review. *Health and Social Care in the Community, 25*(5), 1459-1531.

Bloodworth, A., & McNamee, M. (2010). Clean Olympians? Doping and anti-doping: the views of talented young British athletes. *International Journal of Drug Policy, 21*(4), 276–282.

Christiansen, A. V. (2010). "We are not sportsmen, we are professionals": Professionalism, doping and deviance in elite sport. *International Journal of Sport Management and Marketing, 7*(1), 91–103.

Christiansen, A. V., Schmidt Vinther, A., & Liokaftos, D. (2017). Outline of a typology of men's use of anabolic androgenic steroids in fitness and strength training environments. *Drugs: Education, Prevention and Policy, 24*(3), 295-305.

Conrad, P. (2007). *The medicalization of society: On the transformation of human conditions into treatable disorders.* Johns Hopkins University Press.

Crawford, R. (2006). Health as a meaningful social practice. *Health 10*, 401-420.

De Hon, O., Kuipers, H., & van Bottenburg, M. (2015). Prevalence of doping use in elite sports: A review of numbers and methods. *Sports Medicine, 45*(1), 57-69.

Elbe, A. M., & Pitsch, W. (2018). Doping prevalence among Danish elite athletes. *Performance Enhancement & Health, 6*(1), 28-32.

Henning, A., & Dimeo, P. (2014). The complexities of anti-doping violations: A case study of sanctioned cases in all performance levels of USA cycling. *Performance Enhancement and Health, 3*(3-4), 159-166.

Johnston, L. D., Miech, R. A., O'Malley, P. M., Bachman, J. G., Schulenberg, J. E., & Patrick, M. E. (2018). *Monitoring the future national survey results on drug use: 1975–2017—Overview, key findings on adolescent drug use.* Institute for Social Research, The University of Michigan.

Kartakoullis, N. L., Phellas, C., Pouloukas, S., Petrou, M., & Loizou, C. (2008). The use of anabolic steroids and other prohibited substances by gym enthusiasts in Cyprus. *International Review for the Sociology of Sport, 43*(3), 271–287.

Lucidi, F., Zelli, A., Mallia, L., Grano, C., Russo, P., & Violani, C. (2008). The social-cognitive mechanisms regulating adolescents´ use of doping substances. *Journal of Sports Sciences, 26*(5), 447-456.

Outram, S. M., & Stewart, B. (2015). Condemning and sondoning: Elite amateur cyclists' perspectives on drug use and professional cycling. *International Journal of Drug Policy, 26*(7), 682-687.

Pope, H. G., Kanayama, G., Athey, A., Ryan, E., Hudson, J. I., & Baggish, A. (2014). The lifetime prevalence of anabolic-androgenic steroid use and dependence in Americans: Current best estimates. *The American Journal on Addictions, 23*(4), 371–377.

Sagoe, D., Molde, H., Andreassen, C.S., Torsheim, T., & Pallesen, S. (2014). The global epidemiology of anabolic-androgenic steroid use: a meta-analysis and meta-regression analysis. *Annals of Epidemiology, 24*(5), 383-398.

Swedish National Institute of Public Health. (2011). *Dopning i Samhället [Doping in society].* Statens Folkhälsoinstitut.Ulrich, R., Pope, H. G., Cléret, L., Petróczi, A., Nepusz, T., Schaffer, J., et al. (2018). Doping in two elite athletics competitions assessed by randomized-response surveys. *Sports Medicine, 48*(1), 211–219.

Chapter 4

Women's Gender-Bending in Man-Spreading Cultures

Divisions between doping-related notions limit our ability to understand doping as both a practice and a phenomenon. In the previous two chapters we focused on the relationship between the sports and fitness contexts, both from a historical perspective and through users' experiences. In this chapter and the next, we turn to two other seemingly dichotomous pairs: masculine/feminine and online/offline. As before, we consider the movements between these conceptual pairs: how women negotiate gendered ideals around bodies, doping practices, and cultures, as well as the interface between online/offline contexts. Challenging these divides is necessary for our understanding of women's fitness doping and their doping trajectories, as the relationship between doping and gender is usually positioned in the literature as a subcultural phenomenon with strong relationships to men and masculinity (Christiansen, 2020; Zahnow et al., 2018). In the fitness context, scholars have debated for decades how predominantly young men aim to construct masculinity through pumping iron and developing bulging muscles. In the classic *Little Big Men* study, Klein (1993) showed how men aimed to project external bigness to handle feelings of inner smallness and insecurity. Since then, numerous studies have echoed, in different ways and to different extents, this line of argument and narrative. Bilgrei (2018), for example, showed how doping users in an online forum reported their personal experiences with drugs and how these were described as formative for their lifestyles/trajectories. The style of interaction was referred to as a development of "broscience," a portmanteau of "brother" and "science." This describes a drug/doping culture through which not only doping knowledge is disseminated within a group, but also hegemonic understandings of this practice in terms of its gendered meanings (see Connell & Messerschmidt, 2005; Sumnall et al., 2011). We will further consider the doping-masculinity link in the next chapter.

Monaghan (2001) suggested that the social surroundings and ideals promoted in drug use environments are key to understanding the presence of IPEDs (cf. Pedersen, 2010). Within these types of social communities, women have historically been excluded, or at least relegated to a rear seat (Roussel & Griffet, 2000; Thualagant, 2012; Van Hout & Hearne, 2016). The focus when women's experiences have been addressed has mainly been on female bodybuilders, who have been seen as both an *avant-garde* for female liberation and something exotic or strange.

> Critical feminists, postmodernists, and sport sociologists describe how female bodybuilders balance contradictory demands of muscular

> development versus expectations of normative femininity. These include regulating muscular size to avoid being labeled as 'too big,' 'mannish,' or lesbian (...) using body technologies such as breast enlargements, plastic surgeries, and feminizing hairstyles, outfits, and accessories to counteract 'masculinizing' effects of steroid use or loss of breast tissue. (McGrath & Chananie-Hill, 2009, p. 237)

Although doping, not least in fitness contexts, may still be understood in terms of hegemonic and homosocial patterns – with men dominating the scene and setting the agenda for the practice – studies indicate a growing trend of women (not only female bodybuilders) gradually becoming integrated into doping communities and demanding a cultural space of their own. The result is that the spatiality and gendered dimensions of doping demographics are set in motion (Andreasson & Johansson, 2020). This breaks with what Bunsell (2013) described as a "veil of secrecy" and a "taboo" surrounding women's experiences that lead them to be stigmatized and understood as bound to others' guidance (usually men) in their doping practices. Women are gradually engaging in the practice on their own terms, however, gaining their own use experiences and to some extent challenging the links between and values around masculinity and doping/muscles. This was highlighted in a study of women dopers by Sverkersson et al. (2020) that discussed the potential development of a "sis-science" – an ethnopharmacological culture in which women discuss harm reduction, risk, and the potential potencies of various drugs. They also share knowledge relevant to female biology and negotiate their own experiences and bodies relative to various gendered positions (see also Henning & Andreasson, 2019).

In order to understand the potential impacts a changing doping demography may have in relation to issues such as power, spatiality, culture, and health, we need to look at the gendered dimensions of this practice from women's perspectives and experiences. Women are clearly using IPEDs, although not necessarily in the same ways or for the same reasons as men. In this chapter, we analyze women's own narratives of doping, using discussions from both interview material and data collected from the online platform *ThinkSteroids*. More precisely, we look at how doping practices are approached and understood among women and in relation to gender and hegemonic conceptualizations of doping practices. Further, we also aim to investigate and understand the *thresholding emancipation* (or empowerment) of women's (doped) bodies and drug using experiences (Bladh, 2020). The term threshold, as Bladh uses the concept, reveals how the social and material can serve to impede (gendered) bodies in different ways. Such thresholds are usually made invisible through a neoliberal trope that it is merely down to individual choice (to engage in a community and to dope, for example), but that such choices and steps are by no means as straightforward as they might appear (ibid). Through this, we also dissect and call the meanings attached to women's use of IPEDs into question.

In the next section we explain some of the analytical tools we used in our analysis. Then we present a personal portrait of one user and the particularity of her trajectory that point towards both complicity with gendered norms and the desire to transgress them. Following that is a thematic section focusing on excerpts posted by women on a forum called "Women and Steroids," found on the *ThinkSteroids* platform. We examine how this online space is negotiated by both male and female members. After this, we consider a separate forum designated as women-only and what possibilities this may bring for women, their voices, and their experiences within a male-dominated virtual space. Finally, we conclude with a discussion of what these new demographies and opportunities mean for fitness doping in general and for women in particular. As with the previous chapter, the findings presented here derive from data gathered through ethnographic and nethnographic fieldwork (see Appendix for further information).

Hegemonic Masculinity, Emphasized Femininity, and Beyond

In this chapter we predominantly, but not exclusively, analyze how women negotiate their use of IPEDs in an online context. We understand engaging in doping (both in an online forum and offline) as being or becoming part of a *community of practice* (CofP), which is a group of people who come together with the particular endeavor to do things (practices) (Eckert & McConnell-Ginet, 1992, p. 64). Although we can only examine one aspect of the actual CofP through online discussions, we argue that online spaces can be understood as places where experiences are shared and ideas debated among members. One important characteristic of a CofP is that it does not assume role homogeneity, but rather houses diverse understandings of the particular practice in focus and being *done*. Meaning-making of (drug use) practices can, according to Bundon (2018, p. 279), "contribute to collective understandings of how gender relations operate" but, as we suggest, these understandings are always debated among members in a relational way. They are collectively established, but they are also contested by members and reconceptualized over time within the community.

One way to approach the gendering of doping use within a CofP is to dissect the whole phenomenon in relation to the concept of hegemonic masculinity (Henning & Andreasson, 2019). Introduced by Connell (1987, 1995) this concept has become a central component of gender theory and scholarship (Schippers, 2007).

> Hegemonic masculinity is constructed in relation to women and to subordinated masculinities. These other masculinities need not be as clearly defined – indeed, achieving hegemony may consist precisely in preventing alternatives gaining cultural definition and recognition as alternatives, confining them to ghettos, to privacy, to unconsciousness. (Connell, 1987, p. 186)

This cultural structure or pattern of masculine dominance is dynamic and focuses on the relationship between groups of men and women. According to Connell (1990) hegemonic masculinity is always, in a way, contested. Gender relations are situated within an arena of tension and conflict (Connell & Messerschmidt, 2005). Hegemony does not mean the total oppression of women, however. On the contrary, women may very well understand and accept hegemonic patterns. Due to this, there may be, at times, a more or less perfect match or alliance between hegemonic masculinity and *emphasized femininity*, which refers to how some women quite willingly accommodate the interests and desires of men (see Henning & Andreasson, 2019).

> The concept of emphasised femininity captures a femininity that is particularly strong and can create recognition and legitimacy for women even as it is based in subordination. Femininity is manifest in bodily expressions, words, and actions. Women who come close to an emphasised femininity articulate a distinct femininity based on heterosexuality and subordination. This reflects the idea of desirable femininity and creates certain beliefs about how a woman should be (Connell & Messerschmidt, 2005, p. 688).

Emphasized femininity is based on the acceptance of women's subordination, making it difficult to challenge gender structures from this position. Women can obtain a certain amount of power by demonstrating this form of femininity, but doing so will never really threaten the power relations between men and women (ibid). Such a strategy of conformity to heterosexual norms of attraction, however, stands in stark contrast to other subversive forms of resistance.

To deepen the analysis in this chapter and capture expressions of resistance, we also look to the work of Judith Butler. According to Butler (1990; 2005), terms such as masculine and feminine are historical constructs. This means they are changeable categories always in a process of being made, remade, and redefined. Although the concept of emphasized femininity is still highly relevant in contemporary mass culture, gender hierarchies are "also impacted by new configurations of women's identity and practice" (Connell & Messerschmidt, 2005, p. 848). Through analyzing women's doping experiences, we can explore the dynamic relationship between how women navigate a practice painted in masculine ideals (doing and discussing doping within a particular CofP), and how their negotiations are linked to more general cultural and social structures of gender and gender hierarchies. This, at times, reshapes the content of online doping forums and how gender is enacted within them (Henning & Andreasson, 2019). It is when new/challenging configurations and understandings emerge, even if only suggested or imagined, that previously gendered ideals and practices can begin to be challenged. Following Butler (2005, p. 29), "[f]antasy is what allows us to imagine ourselves and others otherwise; it establishes the possible in excess of the real; it points elsewhere, and when it is embodied, it brings the elsewhere home." Inspired by these words we now direct our attention to one of the women we met during ethnographic fieldwork and zoom in on her personal experiences of IPED use. We pay particular attention to how her lifestyle choices, in diverse ways, have come to raise issues and questions concerning gender.

Not a Grey Housewife

Jannice is a 36-year-old woman who works as a hospital nurse. In her spare time, she is usually found at her local gym. She was previously involved in equestrian sports, but for the past ten years her evening workouts have occupied her mind and time. Her training routine has been a bit off and on over the years, however.

> Then I met this guy and we had a child. And when I became a parent it was bit of an interruption to my lifestyle. But then I gradually got back on track. I went out running with the pram and did push-ups with her on my back and sit ups with her on my stomach. I mean, just to get it going again. Then I snuck in the gym workouts again and got back to my gym. And I noticed that my body enjoyed it, I had really good results and then I became even more motivated. But I had to stop riding, because when you are building muscles you are building the wrong muscles to ride, so to speak. So that was a choice I had to make, and I was riding instructor at the time so it was not that obvious. But that was how it was anyway.

Initially her interest in gym, fitness, and building muscles was only a hobby but it soon became a lifestyle, and her athletic ambitions also came to impact other aspects of her life. A few years ago, she participated in her first amateur competition in the *women's physique* category and she did "okay, although I did not win." Since then she has competed a couple more times. Jannice talked about her body and how her interest in muscle building has changed her perspective on herself and what she considered the ideal life.

> I mean, I like this body quite a bit, especially when I get really muscular. I enjoy feeling strong, to feel my body after a session, the pump and your body is loaded, so to speak. I like it. I don't like to feel empty and flat, and that when someone says "you are thin" it's really nice. No, I don't like that. I want to be big and strong. I kinda felt that I could have had the kids, the house, being a housewife. But I don't wanna be the grey housewife. It's not me. I'm more like, if everybody else wears black, I go for red.

Jannice's narrative is not only about training and the muscular body. It is also an expression of how she positions herself in relation to a narrowly defined and experienced gender order, in which men and women are expected to embrace different positions in the division of labor between the sexes. The gender order she described is only too familiar. She accounted for how the notion of emphasized femininity can almost become a recipe with a long list of ingredients for achieving respectability (Skeggs, 1997) or trustworthiness that women are expected to embody. Jannice, however, did not want to be or become the grey housewife that she sometimes felt was expected of her. Jannice clearly understood, and was potentially on a path to conform to, these expectations. But as she gained more experience in the gym and her goals shifted to include a stronger and more muscular physique, she recalibrated her views and moved towards practices that challenge assumptions around femininity.

Jannice continued to talk about this and about her role models in training. She talked about training films that she sometimes looks at to find inspiration for new workout routines.

> There aren't that many movies with ladies and such. I mean, my role model would be like classical, Ronny Coleman, big boys, I´m sorry to say. The boys do their workouts more like I train. There are no real videos with girls who lift heavily. Or it's not that common anyway. Girls are more aiming to look really feminine. You know, the tight hips and the big boobs, lifting silver weights and all that. You are almost supposed to look like a little fairy even though you are quite muscular. It's almost like nobody wants to explain how I got them [muscles], and the only way is to do it the heavy way. It's almost taboo, and you try to increase the testo as naturally as possible, but perhaps it's not 100 percent perfect for girls.

Jannice's experiences give a certain insight into negotiating the expectations put on her as a woman. She was aware of the type of (emphasized) femininity commonly adopted and portrayed by women in the fitness industry. The assumption that this is what all women strive for is rooted in hegemonic masculinity and related expectations that women view embodying the opposite as the ideal. Jannice challenged this through her own training and with her own muscular body and trajectory towards IPED use. Indeed, she was comfortable with her body and her more "masculine" approach to training. Despite this, she was still confronted with gendered expectations and must continuously resist or challenge such notions. Her narrative underscores how hegemonic masculinity can work and impact individual lifestyles, perceptions of bodies, and practices. In the next two sections we move to the online arena to look at how this kind of gender tension functions in an online context and how it may be perforated and transgressed.

Contesting Cultural Man-Spreading

To further understand women's experiences, we turn back to *ThinkSteroids* and the online community we first discussed in chapter 3. While the personal information presented about the users of this platform is somewhat limited, we can infer that the majority of the posts are by men. Discussion topics can range from a general "Steroid Forum" to a focused "Steroid Homebrew" forum for users making their own steroid products. Until recently there was only one forum on *ThinkSteroids* that focused on women, called "Women and Steroids." Here, we look at the discussions taking place on this forum, which was open to both men and women (although oriented around questions understood as "women issues").[2] In the section that follows we then consider a newly introduced "women-only forum," where only women are allowed to participate.

Perhaps unsurprisingly, women posting on the "Women and Steroids" forum were generally giving and/or requesting information on steroid use. Besides discussing their motives, plans, and goals, several women on the forum were also open to experimenting with new substances. One interesting phenomenon throughout the threads, and in relation to this, was the presence of men's voices. Although this sub-forum was explicitly directed towards women and steroids, men regularly posted in several different capacities. Some answered questions posed by women, especially when no women quickly offered a response. Most common, however, were men posting on behalf of women who were usually their girlfriends or wives. For example, this exchange between two men conversing about their partners.

> Okay so my chick is gonna do a cycle, and I was wondering, what would be more effective, and also SAFE? (In terms of sides, virilization, etc.) Our options are injectable Primobolan Acetate and nandrolone phenyl propionate. Maybe test prop but I'm leaning toward the others instead. I have a large amount of lab grade MCT oil to cut the primo (bad PIP). But any input is appreciated. She's trying to get stronger and build muscle, while minimizing fat/burning fat. (MRmyChick)

Addressing the above excerpt, MRmyChick received the following answer.

> My girl has done both plus Anavar. This her first cycle? I actually think 20 mg of Anavar a day for 6 weeks is a great first or repeat cycle for ladies. (AnavarCycle)

MRmyChick posted a question seemingly on behalf of his partner – his "chick" – who wanted to try steroids. Besides the fact that this discussion can be situated within a misogynistic discourse and a cultural landscape of dominant masculinity, the excerpts indicate that MRmyChick had some knowledge about cycling and products but was seeking out woman-specific information. He uses the phrase "our options" to discuss potential products, intimating that the use and decisions around it are a joint effort and endeavor. He described the goals of getting stronger and reducing fat as belonging solely to her, but that the means were shared. While the goal was hers, they will achieve it together or perhaps she will achieve it (only) through his guidance and support. The received response was similar, exemplifying the split between the man posting and the woman's experience he discussed. It is unclear where the line of

---

[2] The argument presented in this section builds on a previous article published in the journal *Communication & Sport* (Henning & Andreasson, 2019).

experience lies, as AnavarCycle notes his "girl" has used several products but then pivoted to his view of what was best without indicating on what this opinion was based. That he referenced a woman's experience is almost a way of legitimizing his occupancy of this nominally woman's space. Her voice and experience were present but backgrounded relative to his views of what works best for women in general.

Men generally appeared to want to be helpful and encouraging to women in the forum. At the same time, men monopolized the threads and took over this online space initiated for and dedicated to women. This engagement between men on discussion threads within the women's forum was not uncommon, and the majority of threads had more posts from men than women. We do not know why the women MRmyChick and AnavarCycle discussed did not engage directly with one another, but the result was that the experiences of these women and others were present only through their partners (men's voices). Their first-hand capabilities and expertise were then filtered through those of men who have their own views and opinions based on their own experiences of drug use and of their experience of a woman's use. This pattern of men speaking for women or engaging in their place is highlighted in this thread on menstruation.

> Hey guys, my girlfriend started her first cycle of Anavar 7 weeks ago. After about 2 weeks, she had her first period which she said was light but lasted about a week and a half. A couple days ago she began her period again and says it's very light. Were wondering if this is normal or should we be concerned if this is actually Anavar. It did come from a source on here that seems to be very trusted and has been for a few years now. So any feedback and or advice would be greatly appreciated. (PeriodConcerns)

PeriodConcerns soon received responses from two other community members.

> First time on Var? I've had friends completely miss theirs for months on and after Anavar. The level of interference with the estrogen/progesterone cycles, I assume, would vary person to person like the responses to other drugs. (LightORnot)

> Anavar has given my wife the full range of periods. No periods, frequent light periods and even occasional heavy periods with no specific patterns of occurrence. (MrPill)

Incredibly, this entire thread contained no posts from women or anyone claiming to have experienced menstruation. The men described their partners' experiences but were limited in what they could describe and relay: "heavy" and "light" had no relative context here, and the men were unable to supply it. While men may indeed be knowledgeable about topics like menstruation, women's hormones, and reactions to anabolic substances, these men were claiming no expertise on the topic apart from their proximity to women who use or have used this particular substance. Women's voices were missing from this thread, having been supplanted by male users, seemingly without the men noting that women were absent. This absence did not always go unnoticed however, as in this case where user MyFriend referred a woman user to another woman he knew had experience and could give good advice on anabolic use.

> @Barbara I am so glad you posted this question! My friend @Lisa may be able to help you with this. She has been very helpful with my wife's AAS usage. Lots of experience on her end with PEDS. Good luck to you. (MyFriend)

MyFriend's referring a woman user to a knowledgeable woman rather than responding himself maintained the online space for women. It also reinforced that women can be and are experienced, knowledgeable sources of information regarding anabolic use. There was still an element of male centrism and hegemony, as MyFriend seemed to vouch for Lisa's expertise in a way that suggests if Barbara had just replied directly she may not have been viewed as credible. Women were aware of the cultural man-spreading happening on the forum, in which men pushed into the women's area leaving little space for women's voices and experiences. Some clearly expressed a desire for more women to take part in the Women's sub-forum. User NewGoals posted this message in response to a woman participant posting that she was going to share her use and training log.

> Yay, another lady starting a log! welcome!
>
> you look fantastic! I'm currently dieting down for a show in 8 weeks and am going through what you mentioned above (massive hunger, low energy and brain fog). I think this will be my last show, and then I will switch to something like you're doing now (building in the winter & cutting in the spring). (NewGoals)

The excitement in this post underscores the lack of women using the dedicated forum space. Similar comments were not found in the general forums often dominated by men, as men sharing their logs was routine (see Andreasson & Johansson, 2017). Similarly, one woman user, Sam, posted this into a thread in which another new woman had received some sexually suggestive comments from men on the site: "It would be [sic] nice to keep some women here…" Sam was concerned the aggressive messages would cause the new woman to leave the forum altogether after the men's comments had begun to take over the thread. To this end, and seemingly paradoxically to its intent of creating a space for female users, the *Women & Steroids* forum was largely a forum in which knowledge, experience, and the ability to talk and discuss doping was filtered through hegemonic conceptualizations of masculinity and men's experiences and knowledge.

New Frontiers?

As a result of "the shortcomings addressed" in the previous section (read: men's tendency to background women's voices; see also Henning & Andreasson, 2019), as well as "female member feedback," *ThinkSteroids* explained in the spring of 2020 that they had decided to open up a new forum called "Women's Steroid Experiences." This forum is exclusively dedicated to posts by women.[3] It is thus a women-only forum in which men are not allowed to engage in discussions. The following notice appeared on their website announcing the new sub-forum.

> Effectively immediately, the "Women's Steroid Experiences" subforum permissions will only allow women's participation to POST NEW THREADS and RESPOND to EXISTING THREADS.
> The "Women's Steroid Experiences" subforum is a dedicated space for WOMEN ONLY to engage, discuss, and share their steroid experiences with other women.
> A new second subforum was created in the women's section tentatively called "Women and Steroids Open to Everyone". This subforum was created in recognition of the fact that some women specifically welcome feedback from both men and women, some men seek feedback from women who have used steroids, and both men and women can contribute to the knowledgebase in this area. (TheHost)

Whereas the need for an exclusive forum for women only was debated among the members when this news was presented on *ThinkSteroids*, most seemed in favor of the changes made and the potential benefits they could accommodate. Taking into consideration that there are quite a few men who are supportive of women's experiences and approach the forum in a reasonable way, the members decided to keep this door open with the "all are welcome" forum on "Women and Steroids" discussed in the previous section.

Building on the previous section, we look at some of the discussions around the changes made and how they were understood by both men and women members. We also look at the texture and content of the new women-only forum as it was introduced and discussions began. We start, however, with one member responding to the rationale for keeping dual sub-forums as presented above by TheHost. Here a male member explained his approach to discussions on women and steroids.

---

[3] The argument presented in this section builds on a previous article published in the journal *Communication & Sport* (Andreasson & Henning, 2021).

> I'm glad there is still the option for both sexes to participate together. I've reached out (and plenty of other members have as well) to female members because of questions that pertain to my wife. I wouldn't have had a way to ask another woman about these things discretely (...) I also agree with creating a female only area and applaud the decision. We had a female introduce herself just this week, and low and behold one of the first members to say hello had been previously banned for sexually harassing a female member. Wonder how long it'll take for him to do it again? That is a picture perfect and crystal clear reason as to why this plattform would benefit by that section. (MrWonder)

Although we do not know why MrWonder's wife (MrsWonder?) does not ask the questions herself instead of him asking them for/about her, this seems to be a quite straightforward approach to the rationale for keeping both forums (dual spaces). Due to this, forum members, regardless of gender, can discuss issues concerning harm reduction while still allowing women to opt out of the all-comers forum for potential sexual harassment or other reasons. Another member talked about this and the women-only forum in terms of creating ripples on the water, as previous members who appeared to have left the community can now get "back in the game."

> Looks like some ladies came out of the woodworks since the change. I haven't seen @Laura post in a long time. Glad to see some of the ladies making their way back to the site. (JosieLifts)

> I think this is a good direction to go in (...) so you boys stay at bay and behave but still can read our posts. It won't get cluttered with unnecessary posts. It's our own little section where we can say and ask anything and know there's only female feedback coming.
>
> It's a good move. We just need the ladies back again! (MuscleEmpress)

In a way, these women are pursuing the possibility of breaking the connection between doping and male hegemony, although in a secluded space. There are several posts from both men and women in favor of this approach and forming vocabularies of justification in terms of not only uninterrupted discussions on ethnopharmacological female bodily responses, but also as a means of bracketing the previous and occasionally occurring heteronormative and misogynistic responses made by some men on the all-comers forum. Seemingly as a result, old (and new) women members found their way back to the newly introduced women-only forum to engage in discussions. MuscleEmpress added a layer of complexity, however, in her acknowledgement that though this new forum is to be used by women only, men are still able to read the discussions. In theory, at least, they are freed from men's interference, but their experiences on the forum are still potentially subject to male surveillance. This may have implications for how individual women choose to present and legitimate themselves relative to men's silent observations.

Some women are actively working to build up their community and collective experience-based knowledge through their own posts. One member presented an extensive report on her current course and described which drugs she uses, their effects, and reasons for her dosages. She ended her post by describing her motivation for engaging in the forum.

> Mostly posting this for FYI for others. I find there is little information for women and steroids out there. At least real usage and hard truths. (#StrongWomen)

Combined with other members also aiming to contribute to a foundation for a women's ethnopharmacological subculture by presenting their own courses, there were also posts on side effects and risk. Searching for women's first-hand knowledge, some members will ask questions about courses and others then do their best to answer them. Below is an excerpt from a response to a question from a woman asking about her use of Anavar and the side effects she experienced.

> When using var, as I mentioned over and over in my answers to especially women, stomach cramps/pains are mostly dehydration issue as well as protein intake issue. While on var, make sure to increase your lean proteins and water and that will help and most likely eliminate your issues. (IronLifestyle)

Although the women-only forum is not yet that extensive, it is growing. The discussions taking shape also open the possibility for women to set the female body and morphology as the standard and norm for discussion in a way that was previously understood as less likely to occur. This could be partly understood as a way for women to break the historical link between doping and masculinity. In doing so, it becomes increasingly possible for the women to occupy this subcultural space and reconceptualize their use – to stop the cultural man-spread. They are able to discuss their experiences less in terms of gender and more in terms of harm reduction, health, bodily issues, and lifestyle strategies. As such, the women-only forum facilitates a possibility for cultural and contextual recalibration of doping experiences.

Conclusions

Becoming part of a doping CofP can be understood as investing time and diffusing knowledge within the realm of an ethnopharmacological online/offline subculture (cf. Monaghan, 2012). Within this cultural context, methods and theories on drug use, management of courses, and possible side effects are discussed. Further, interests in and experimentation with doping to achieve the desired body, whatever that means for the individual, are vividly debated. In this chapter, we used both a personal portrait of a user and online discussions to unfold the gendered dimensions and implications of such an endeavor. We have not, however, focused on the particularity of individual positions *per se*. Nor have we focused on the ways masculinities and femininities are enacted as identity positions. Instead, we have tried to focus on the subcultural texture or fibers that hold/bring the doping community together and the gendered dimensions of that community. It is the community and the relationships that unfold within that have been the object of study rather than individual participants. This also goes for the case study of Jannice, who in diverse ways negotiated and approached the gendered structuring of muscles, doping, and capable bodies.

Paying attention to the cultural structure of a doping CofP in relation to gender, that is how the "fibers" of the community are imprinted by gendered understandings, we can also see the threshold expectations for women users compared with those for men. For example, *ThinkSteroids* has a Notable Members list that ranks its members on quantity and quality (i.e., number of likes) of use, which is a way of differentiating between members of the broader CofP by conferring status, as well as a form of power, onto some members and their bodies (Henning & Andreasson, 2019). The highest ranked members are more or less exclusively men, which indirectly constitutes them as a type of expert, while newer or lower ranked members – including many of the women members – are situated as laypersons. Following this, it is not surprising that a forum in which men and women can interact about doping practices can also serve to grant some members (men) cultural capital/stamina, while others (women) are more likely to meet high thresholds manifested as corrective comments and limited cultural space. To this end, men's voices and narratives can be said to block women's opportunities to both share and accumulate knowledge and experience, which would then impact their trajectories and practices.

By contrast, a women-only forum can facilitate the possibility of developing a doping CofP based in sis-science (Sverkersson et al., 2020), in which women's doped bodies are debated in relation to health, lifestyle, and women's biology, rather than in terms of heterosexual desirability and emphasized femininity. The development of women-only doping spaces, although still under male surveillance, creates at least a partial opportunity for women to form their own bodily narratives and doping experiences. The lessening of the male hegemony in relation to doping experiences, side effects, and trajectories may present a new frontier for understanding contemporary doping demography. In doing so, women´s doping experiences can be detached from discourses of gender and muscularity, of man-spreading cultures, and be connected instead to discourses focusing on health and harm reduction. This may also impact women's doping trajectories as use is normalized.

The new forum is exclusionary in that men are kept out of the discussions. However, it can also be understood as newly inclusive of women's experiences, knowledge, and bodies in ways different from discussions taking place in the shadow of men's voices, ideals, status, and knowledge. Excluding men's participation opens up an opportunity for women to renegotiate the online space, recenter it around their bodies and experiences, and invest in a collective bank of women's experience and community building, thus bursting through a social threshold. Of course, it is up to women what they do with this new space and it is likely to be mixed. As Jannice's case highlighted, women can change and recreate their own narratives, through a process of cumulative cultural recalibration, though these necessarily exist alongside lived experience and self-identity. When we account for these more personal factors, we also blur the line between challenging and reinforcing hegemonic gender ideals as well as fantasy/lived experiences and understandings of the gender of doping. This discussion will be further developed in the next chapter.

REFERENCES

Andreasson, J., & Henning, A. (2021). Challenging hegemony through narrative: Centering women´s experiences and establishing a sis-science culture through a women-only doping forum. *Communication & Sport*. Advance online publication. DOI: 10.1177/21674795211000657

Andreasson, J., & Johansson, T. (2020). *Fitness doping. Trajectories, gender, bodies and health*. Palgrave Macmillan.

Andreasson, J., & Johansson, T. (2017). Doped manhood. Negotiating fitness doping and masculinity in an online community. In C. Haywood & T. Johansson (Eds.), *Marginalized masculinities: Contexts, continuities and change* (pp. 139–154). Routledge.

Bladh, G. (2020). *Thresholding emancipation: Bodies within the vicinities of gym and fitness*. Idrottsforum.org

Bilgrei, O.R. (2018). Broscience: Creating trust in online drug communities. *New Media and Society*, *20*(8), 2712–27.

Bundon, A. (2018). Blogging and feminist participatory research online. In L. Mansfield., J. Caudwell., B. Wheaton., & B. Watson (Eds.), *The Palgrave handbook of feminism and sport, leisure and physical education* (pp. 275–292). Palgrave Macmillan.

Bunsell, T. (2013). *Strong and hard Women*. Routledge.

Butler, J. (1990). *Gender trouble: Feminism and the subversion of identity*. Routledge.

Butler, J. (2005). *Undoing gender*. Routledge.

Christiansen, A. V. (2020). *Gym culture, identity and performance-enhancing drugs: Tracing a typology of steroid use*. Routledge.

Connell, R. W. (1987). *Gender & power*. Polity Press.

Connell, R. W. (1995). *Masculinities*. Polity Press.

Connell, R. W., & Messerschmidt, J. (2005). Hegemonic masculinity: Rethinking the concept. *Gender & Society*, *19*(6), 829–859.

Connell, R.W. (1990) An iron man: The body and some contradictions of hegemonic masculinity. In M. Messner & D. Sabo (Eds.), *Sport, men and the gender order. Critical Feminist Perspectives*. Human Kinetic Books.

Eckert, P., & McConnell-Ginet, S. (1992). Think practically and look locally: Language and gender as community-based practice. *Annual Review of Anthropology*, *21*(1), 461–490.

Henning, A., & Andreasson, J. (2019). "Yay, another lady starting a log!" Women's fitness doping and the gendered space of an online doping forum. *Communication & Sport*. Advance online publication. *DOI: 10.1177/2167479519896326*

Klein, A. (1993). *Little big men: Bodybuilding, subculture and gender construction*. New York: State University of New York Press.

McGrath, S., & Chananie-Hill, R. (2009). 'Big Freaky-Looking Women': Normalizing gender transgression through bodybuilding. *Sociology of Sport Journal*, *26*(2), 235–254.

Monaghan, L. F. (2001). *Bodybuilding, drugs and risk: Health, risk and society*. Routledge.

Monaghan, L. F. (2012). Accounting for illicit steroid use. Bodybuilders' justifications. In A. Locks & N. Richardson. (Eds.). *Critical readings in bodybuilding*. Routledge.

Pedersen, I. K. (2010). Doping and the perfect body expert: Social and cultural indicators of performance-enhancing drug use in Danish gyms. *Sport in Society*, *13*(3), 503–516.

Roussel, P., & Griffet, J. (2000). The path chosen by female bodybuilders: A tentative interpretation. *Sociology of Sport Journal*, *17*(2), 130–50.

Schippers, M. (2007). Recovering the feminine other: Masculinity, femininity, and gender hegemony. *Theory and Society*, *36*(1), 85–102

Skeggs, B. (1997). *Formations of class and gender: Becoming respectable*. Sage.

Sumnall, H., Evans-Brown, M., & McVeigh, J. (2011). Social, policy, and public health perspectives on new psychoactive substances. *Drug Testing and Analysis*, *3*(7-8), 515–523.

Sverkersson, E., Andreasson, J., & Johansson, T. (2020). 'Sis science' and fitness doping. Ethnopharmacology, gender and risk. *Social Sciences*, *9*(4), 1-13.

Thualagant, N. (2012). The conceptualization of fitness doping and its limitations. *Sport in Society: Cultures, Commerce, Media, Politics*, *15*(3), 409–19.

Van Hout, M-C., & Hearne, E. (2016). Netnography of female use of the synthetic growth hormone CJC-1295: Pulses and potions. *Substance Use & Misuse, 51*(1), 73–84.
Zahnow, R., McVeigh, J., Bates, G., Hope, V., Kean, J., Campbell, J., & Smith, J. (2018). Identifying a typology of men who use anabolic androgenic steroids (AAS). *International Journal of Drug Policy, 55*, 105–112.

Chapter 5

Sex, Drugs, and Muscles: "Welcome to Planet Porno"

That the desire to improve one's appearance and social status is one of the most important factors in men's engagement in fitness doping, which usually means aiming for bigger muscles in line with prevailing norms of heteronormative masculinity, has been repeatedly underscored by researchers (Christiansen, 2020; Klein, 1993; Parkinson & Evans, 2006). In fact, the link between muscularity and virility has been visible in both mainstream and bodybuilding subcultures for decades. For example, in the iconic bodybuilding documentary *Pumping Iron* bodybuilding icon Arnold Schwarzenegger described the feeling of pumped-up muscles as the most satisfying one can have (Gaines & Butler, 1974; Schwarzenegger & Petre, 2012). *Pumping Iron* also featured Schwarzenegger talking about muscle-building practices and life in the gym – specifically about the experience of *the pump* – in terms of a continuous orgasm. Thus, the distinction between pumped-up (and doped) muscles on the one hand and masculinity and sexual ability/virility on the other, was anything but watertight. Through such accounts we can see the historical continuity of how pumped muscles have been and are associated with both steroids and masculinized sexual fantasies and performances.[4]

Despite what may look like a straightforward link (and a contrast to women's experiences as discussed in previous chapter), however, men must also negotiate issues of gender and sexuality within gym and doping subcultures, as well as within their daily lives and interpersonal relationships. In this chapter, we focus on men bodybuilders' fitness doping experiences. More precisely, this chapter aims to explore the connections between bodybuilding, (hyper)masculinity, sexuality, and the construction of subcultural and sexual spaces. Through our analysis we call into question some of the lines drawn between notions of deviant/idealized bodies, pleasure/harm, and fantasy/lived experience. By interrogating these divisions we can better understand how gender intersects with men's understandings of sexuality and questions concerning intimacy and relationships (Andreasson & Johansson, 2020).

In the next section we explain some of the central approaches and concepts we applied in our analysis, building on those used in the previous chapter. From there we look at accounts from two groups of male IPED users in tandem. The first is a group of Swedish gym-goers and bodybuilders who discussed their fitness doping

[4] This chapter builds on an article previously published in the *Journal of Bodies, Sexualities, and Masculinites* (Andreasson & Johansson, 2021).

experiences. These narratives were gatherered through ethnographic fieldwork, mainly consisting of interviews and observations. The second accounts are from *ThinkSteroids*, the online fitness doping platform also analyzed in previous chapters (see Appendix on method and methodology). We draw on these combined data to explore how these men understand their muscular bodies relative to notions of masculinity, their experiences and perceptions of sex related to steroid use, and how interpersonal relationships can be affected by doping. Through this we explore how male fitness dopers negotiate between different, and sometimes conflicting, masculinities.

Pleasure, Harm, and Masculinities

Although scholars have discussed the intertwined nature of muscularity, masculinity, and sexual virility enhanced through fitness doping – which points to a cultural and historical continuity of the symbolism attached to steroids and their effects – this field of knowledge and discourses on steroid use have been dominated by the "narrative of harm" (Mulrooney et al., 2019). In relation to gender, steroid use has often been discussed in terms of hypermasculinity and men exhibiting violent behavior (Bach, 2005; Christiansen, 2020; Denham, 2008; Jordan-Young & Karkazis, 2019). There is, however, a growing body of research suggesting that there is substantial variation among steroid-using populations in motivations for use, how individuals understand their own motives, and the effects and transformative nature of the drugs (Begley et al., 2017; Christiansen et al., 2017; Underwood, 2017). Mulrooney et al. (2019) discussed the need to consider use not only from a harm narrative perspective, but also in terms of recreation and pleasure:

> In addition to the delayed gratification which comes from body/performance modification, it is not unusual for users to report pleasurable feelings such as increased libido, greater confidence and increased wellbeing and strength (…) Given the centrality of pleasure for many users in the consumption of these substances, pleasure is an essential part of a coherent and reasoned response to steroid consumption. (p. 3)

Still, research has paid little attention to the pleasures of fitness doping. In a study on bodybuilding and IPED use, Underwood (2017) showed how the community's participants aimed for a shredded body (muscular and ultra-lean) in order to appeal to the general public, hoping to gain social benefits such as dominance over "beta males" and women (see also Kimergård, 2015). In this way, IPEDs were understood as a central component of a lifestyle dedicated not only to making the individual more sexually active and attractive, but also to having an impact on gendered power relations (Monaghan, 2001). Community members not only negotiated homosocial relations, hypermasculinity, and bodies, but also lifestyle issues concerning sexual libido, social status, and health.

In this chapter we are interested in how dynamic and mobile relationships between different groups of men and women are played out. Particular gendered understandings and the gendering of certain practices, such as the use of IPEDs, are seen as inevitably situated in arenas of tensions and conflicts, and in terms of masculinity configurations we are interested in the reconfigurations of hegemonic masculinity in between stability and change. Through studying an often marginalized and subcultural masculinity, that is bodybuilders, we hope to contribute to the wider discussion on hegemonic masculinity in transition. We also use the concept of *pornification* – the tendency to absorb sexual imaginaries from the porn industry into mainstream culture and everyday life – to analyze how sexuality is constructed in bodybuilding culture, in this case with the help of steroids and other muscle-building IPEDs (cf. Kammeyer, 2008).

Of course, there is an ongoing discussion about redefining and reconfiguring masculinity, mainly tied to the wider theoretical project of analyzing different masculinities in relation to *hegemonic masculinity* (Connell, 1995; 2001; Haywood et al., 2018; Johansson & Ottemo, 2015). Although there is agreement as to what can be seen as a *pluralization of masculinities* – meaning there are different ways of doing masculinity – the debate about how we should define hegemonic masculinity continues (Demetriou, 2001; Haywood et al., 2018; Hearn, 2004; Howson, 2006).

Muscles, Desires, and Consequences

The status of the huge and extraordinary male body of the bodybuilder has changed over the years. In the 1990s and early 2000s, the negative effects of steroids were heavily debated (Andreasson & Johansson, 2014). As a result, bodybuilding and bodybuilders were stigmatized and exiled from the center of the fitness industry and culture to a certain degree. Fast forward to today, however, and there seems to be a new and growing market for bodybuilding. A large number of international on- and offline magazines – such as *Flex Magazine*, *Muscular Development*, *Bodypower*, *Muscle*, and *Musclemag* – are devoted almost entirely to the art of bodybuilding. There are also books and manuals on the market that offer different training programs and advice on how to mold and form a perfect body, in addition to an entire sphere of social media dedicated to the same topic. On a societal level, these extreme bodies, including bodybuilders with huge, muscular bodies, may be seen as grotesque and deviant (McGrath & Chananie-Hill, 2009, Locks & Richardson, 2011). But on a cultural and symbolic level, such bodies are highly valued and seen as expressions of hardcore masculinity (Denham, 2008). Bodybuilders are also quite conscious of the negative views of the sport. The wish to become huge, creating a hyper-muscular masculinity, is therefore often seen as a somewhat ambivalent project and identity pursuit. There is a complex relationship between the objectives created within the subcultural space – where huge is perfect – and the reactions obtained in everyday life. This is exemplified in the narrative below, in which John, a former competitive bodybuilder, who currently "only" works out a couple days per week and uses occasional courses of steroids, talked about his prime years. Here the self-perception of the body is addressed as a somewhat problematic and almost dissociative experience.

> There really are mixed feelings to it, the body. Sure, it was great fun showing that you had a well-trained body, but it was also somewhat embarrassing. My girlfriend thought so, too. I know that she didn't like me being that big. Some people really enjoy showing off, though. They just go and lie on the beach because they want to show off. But I never had that. I just wanted to be left alone. The perception of the body can become so damned distorted. There's this video clip, for example, from the U.S. when we were on holiday a couple of years ago. I'm walking towards the camera, on the beach, and my girlfriend is filming. I hadn't seen that clip for a while, and then I saw this fucking guy coming up from the water, this big fucking bastard. I didn't realize it at first, but it was me. (John)

Another participant, Ted, talked about how the doping-enhanced bodybuilding body is perceived, not only by him (as above), but also by others.

> Right now, I'm in pretty decent shape. I am 1.9 m tall and weigh around 135 kilos, so I guess it's pretty obvious that I've been using [steroids]. But I can sit down and have a conversation, and show that I'm pretty normal anyway, you know. You sit down and eat a hamburger and pizza and stuff like that. You're not extreme or fanatical when it comes to diet. You can have a beer and still talk about alcohol problems in general. You can talk about the situation in Afghanistan, gender issues, and things like that. (Ted)

Being aware of public perceptions and expectations that are placed on doped bodies, Ted tries to present himself as an intellectual young man in various ways. Talking about gender issues and equity as well as the situation in Afghanistan can thus be seen as a strategy to counter processes of being defined as the muscular, but not that enlightened, Other. Similarly, MrBig is an online user who posted about his wife's negative response to his quick steroid-boosted physical transformation. He reflected on the way she and others view the built body.

> I think its got to do with what she thinks people think, what people say, and that maybe she doesn't actually like me this big. Doesn't mean she'll leave me for it or make my life hell for it. I can understand women not wanting their men as big as me (I get it, I'm only 5'7", but maybe being shorter makes the wider thing more of shock). I was never under any illusion that all women loved bodybuilding body types. (MrBig)

This self-reflective and somewhat ambivalent way of talking about the male body, as illustrated in the comments above, has become quite common in bodybuilding culture (Andreasson & Johansson, 2014; 2020). There is a heightened self-awareness and notions of muscular masculinities are not taken for granted. Instead, they are scrutinized and problematized. One of the online users, MuscleKing, posted a thread in the "General Discussion" forum describing his transition away from both bodybuilding and steroids. In a response post, he clarified some of the reasons he was initially interested in muscle-building, talking about himself and his bodybuilding body in terms of masculinity, expressing a quite conflicted position.

> Yeah a huge part of my obsession with strength and muscle manifested itself in my teen years. I was quiet with a lot of hidden rage from my parents' failures and the failures of the CPS [child protection services] system. I wanted to be larger than life to prove it to who knows…me? My dad? I don't know. To prove I was stronger than him? Protection? I don't know. But being a victim was never gonna happen if I got stronger, right? It gave me a way to feel empowered I've always used it [bodybuilding] as a purge to vent frustration in different stages of my life. It was a hardening tool and a tool of empowerment. Something I used with devastating effectiveness as motivation to get to the next level and then the next. (MuscleKing)

Mirroring previous research, MuscleKing´s narrative exemplifies how some men use steroids to camouflage feelings of smallness and insecurity, by projecting physical bigness and masculinity (Christiansen, 2020; Klein, 1993). Many of the men show this kind of self-reflection around the muscular, male-connoted body, but remain in the gym and bodybuilding culture even so. Consequently, this self-reflective masculinity does not necessarily lead to a redefinition of bodybuilding culture and the body. Instead, in a majority of the narratives, the huge, masculine, hard-core body is still regarded as something desirable. Whereas MuscleKing was a bit hesitant, others were more convinced in their approach and in the meanings attached to the muscular body.

> I believe that it has to do with masculinity. You want to mark or stand your ground let people know that you can defend your position. You know, something like that. It probably varies a lot between different individuals. I'm not extreme in any way, but I'm certainly bigger than most guys. I've benefitted greatly from being big in all my various jobs, especially as a doorman. People always think twice before approaching me, you know. It's hard to pinpoint, but I think I really enjoy being this big. It's satisfying and makes me feel secure. I know that I can take care of myself and my family. If everything goes to hell, I know that I don't need to run for help or call up someone else. I can handle it myself. (Conrad)

Although these men show that it is possible to talk about a self-reflective, muscular masculinity that is evolving in the subcultural space of bodybuilding, this does not mean that the desire to build huge bodies and to do so by whatever means possible has disappeared. Rather, echoing previous research (Christiansen, 2020; Thualagant, 2012), we find here a sort of keynote about a rationalized steroid lifestyle through which the participants aim to transform their bodies and to become/feel masculine and competitive in relation to their peers and partners. Nevertheless, the desire to continuously develop and become more of a man must be negotiated or balanced in relation to potential social stigmatization and/or thoughts about personal capabilities. These intertwined tendencies are clear when looking at how some informants try to "rewrite" and respond to actual or imagined questioning of their lifestyle choices (Andreasson, 2015), arguing for a more intellectual and self-reflective approach to the notion of masculinity. In the next section we look at how steroid use and understandings of masculinity intersect with experiences and thoughts on sex and sexuality.

Negotiating Planet Porno

Although most of the participants mainly discussed their use of steroids in terms of a means to build muscles and create a masculine body, they also mentioned other (side)effects in their narratives. Rupert, for example, who has completed several courses of steroids over the years, explained some emotional effects.

> You mustn't forget that testosterone controls a lot of things in the body. It controls your emotions and sex and joy and sadness. There are, after all, those who have taken too much of it, too high dosages, and they can burst out crying because there's a scratch on the door of their car, or if their shoe gets wrecked. You don't have to cry about that, really. (Rupert)

As explained, steroids can bring a certain emotional sensitivity and awareness that makes the user feel everything more clearly or more strongly when on a course. This sort of heightened awareness/sensitivity is usually thought of and discussed in terms of adjectives describing the self as becoming more of something, such as "focused," "sensitive," "muscular," or "virile." Despite the occasional mention of some negative consequences, these qualities are basically, and at least initially, described as being desired. This seems to be particularly true when it comes to sex and sexual encounters. Another interviewee, Will, talked about the effects of steroids.

> Right on the first day I could feel the vibes in my body purely sexual, you know. I get, I mean, I can go on and on. I become like a fucking rabbit! And my girlfriend said "What the hell! Are you on it again?" And I kind of replied "Yeah, so what?" "I've noticed, since you won't leave me alone for a minute." I could go on doing it 4, 5, 6, 7 times a day, you know? (...) It was

> stressful for her, 'cause I just wanted to fuck all the time. Having sex all the time. (Will)

This heightened lust is sometimes talked about in terms of pleasure and pride: being on steroids "makes women think you are from Planet Porno" as another participant explained. What the participants described was something both pleasurable and exotic a kind of new awareness and curiosity about sex and the body as well as being something partly out of control. One interviewee, Tristan, described this in terms of becoming (like) a teenager again.

> One gets these really twisted and strange thoughts, because of the increased libido, you know. The testosterone just spins, really hard. It's like you're a teenager all over again, and just want to experiment. Like when you're fourteen years old, and you just want to have sex. You have daydreams about having sex with your teacher. It's like a new puberty. All these feelings just come back when you're taking high dosages of testosterone. Quite a lot of people have trouble controlling this. Many (...) I'm not saying that they become homosexual or anything, just that they have problems controlling their sexual feelings. (Tristan)

When these men, like Tristan above, talk about their heightened sexual virility, they are in one sense proud of themselves. Potency and virility are visible bodily indicators of a hard-core masculinity – being ready to perform, again and again. As is having "many sexual relationships – many women. It's a silver lining in life," as explained by another interviewee. Such manifestations of masculinity are also connected to pornographic fantasies of being in control and expressing heteronormative male desires and potency (Mullholland, 2013). They are thus pointing towards an increased sexualisation and *pornification* of their lifestyles following their IPED use, as when Tristan (above) describes sexualized daydreams. At the same time, the men describe the relentless lust almost in a machine-like and technological manner (cf. Garlick, 2016). Sustaining the hard and erect penis is a desired state of the male body, to a certain degree, but the narratives also contain descriptions of unmanageable sexual practices/thoughts – pleasure that can easily shift into harm. Consequently, what we see here is an ambivalent construction of heteronormative masculinity. In some of the narratives, such as this from Matt, loss of control was also a source of worry.

> There are quite a few users who become a kind of sex addict during their testosterone courses. They masturbate frantically. I've heard stories about guys going to the toilet to masturbate before, during and after the work out, you know. Yeah. I've heard about it. It's totally crazy. I am thinking about Ricky Bruch [Former Swedish athlete, known for being outspoken about his drug use in the early 70s]. He was a devoted masturbator throughout his career. He had this constant erection, and had to stand on his head and piss in

> the bathtub. It all depends on the what kind of steroids you take though. Not all kinds of steroids give you a constant erection. There are also steroids leading to an enlarged penis your organ is simply growing. (Matt)

Similarly to the experiences touched upon by Matt and Tristan, the online steroid forums are full of discussions around sex and sex drive. At times, these feelings were discussed in more sexually aggressive ways. For example, one post from a user's training log included a description of the effects of Trenbolone Acetate as increasing his libido and making him feel "I'm about 50% rapist right now to be honest." Another user responded that "Feeling 50% rapist is only good when you're seeing someone or in a relationship. When I am on tren seeing someone it is great. Otherwise it's not good. Lol. The horniness turns into an issue."

Symbolically, the heightened hunger for sex can be seen as an indicator of a hard-core, mythological masculinity, but the lack of control and misogynistic attitude also signals something disturbing for the men and at times blurs the line between fantasy and lived experience, and between pleasure and harm. The narratives and interactions show clear traces of a conflictual heteronormative masculinity. On the one hand, the steroids affect the bodies and create desires that belong in a pornographic fantasy of a perfect male and potent (hetero)sexual ability. On the other hand, the men also expressed feelings of being a victim of their desires and lust. Such feelings were also related to thoughts about what might happen in the aftermath of steroid use, such as testicular atrophy or reduced virility. In the next section we zoom in on the social consequences IPED use.

Fitness Doping Lifestyles and Relationships

Perhaps unsurprisingly, the pornification of the male body, and the machine-like sexuality that is described in previous section, can also result in social and intimate relationship problems. In a "General Discussion" thread on whether or not to hide steroid use from one's partner, HeMan, who is not currently using steroids, offered his view.

> Any girl I've had while using was aware of enhancement but never outright said it or showed them anything cause then it's just a hearsay story when we break up from her point of view. However, if I was to start back in I would only do it if I had full support of who I'm with cause they're gonna have to deal with 4-5 rounds [of sex] a day rather than 1-3 and that's a lot to ask a wee gal so gotta make sure she's ready for that too. (HeMan)

The discussion on disclosure was full of mixed views, ranging from fully hiding use to including partners in doing injections. HeMan's view took into account the effects on one's partner, as he recognized the increased desire for sex in one partner can impact the other. This was underscored in a post by another user, R_Uready, "Bro I'm struggling with this as we speak. And to make it worse my girl hasn't been able to keep up for a while. She says this isn't normal how frequent I can go and how long it goes for. It's like you almost need 3 girls so you're not just destroying 1." Both forum users highlighted the ease with which the line between pleasure (increased sex drive) and harm (out of control sexual urges) for both the self and their partner(s) can be crossed as a result of steroid use. This issue can negatively impact relationships in multiple ways, as one of the interviewees, Matt, explained how he is affected by steroids.

> I tend to visit other women, yeah. It's very common. I have serious problems. When using testosterone, I can't limit myself to just one woman, and this is not at all uncommon. Loads of men have problems staying faithful on steroids. My girlfriend notices that I cannot control myself. I want to have sex, seven or eight times a day, and that's not normal; there are no limits (...) You have to fight together, knowing why it happens, it's a medical issue. It becomes a medical issue. (Matt)

Matt has found it difficult to stay faithful when on steroids. According to him, however, his cheating habits can be explained and dealt with as a medical issue rather than a social one. Nevertheless, it is easy to understand that his way of reasoning would affect feelings of trust in a relationship, and that the use of steroids brings emotional and social challenges.

Another interviewee, Noah, talked about the ways the bodybuilding lifestyle has affected his relationships with women.

> It's a lifestyle. It's simply a whole way of life. Let me tell you, I've had relationships with quite a few women. I've been in a relationship with them and they haven't been able to understand this lifestyle. They think it's strange and they can't deal with it. It's not only about steroids, it's about lifestyle – the way you live. (Noah)

Above, Noah touches on some of the complexities of being in a relationship while simultaneously investing heavily in the bodybuilding lifestyle. Entering into intimate relationships is not easy, as they are sometimes believed to have a potentially negative impact on training and discipline. The solution for some has been to deliberately stay single or to view relationships as necessarily temporary. Another solution is to only invest emotionally in women who are also involved in this subcultural sphere, that is, with a partner who might be competing in, for example, Women's Physique or Body Fitness.

Nevertheless, exemplified in Noah's narrative is an ongoing negotiation between expressed athletic aspirations and the social aspects of everyday life, a pattern also found in sport and usually discussed in terms of the time- and strain-based leisure-work-family conflict (Hambrick et al., 2013; McCarville, 2007). Another interviewee brought up other social side effects and problems.

> Then we have this aggressiveness – that's the scary part of the male hormone, testosterone. And it isn't that surprising that we become more aggressive when we devour artificial male hormones (...) Everybody I know becomes more aggressive that side increases. And obviously this affects everybody. That said, this doesn't mean that all people using steroids become, like, crazy. It's not about that. That's not what I'm suggesting. But one does become more irritable. (Magnus)

What Magnus touches upon in the above excerpt, which was also regularly discussed in threads on the steroid forum, is something that has been debated by scholars for quite a while. What has been called "roid rage" (slang for "steroid rage") is now a more or less established term referring especially, but not exclusively, to young men's aggressive attitudes towards women and other men as a result of their steroid use (Copeland et al., 2000; Monaghan, 2001). In a way, Magnus tried to make a distinction between uncontrolled aggression on the one hand, and increased irritability and edginess on the other. What is clear, however, is how steroids are thought to impact the user's state of mind and that this actually affects everybody around him. In this section, we have seen how steroid-using men negotiate their drug use in relation to questions concerning intimacy, social relations, and family life. The use of IPEDs is simultaneously constructed as a powerful symbol for bodily success and a domineering subcultural masculinity. It is also associated with a feeling that the potential gains could come at too high a cost, socially and relationship-wise.

Conclusion

By considering the interview material with male Swedish bodybuilders and the posts from the *ThinkSteroids* members, in this chapter we have shown how these men experience and understand their (doped) muscular, hyper-masculine bodies. This lifestyle and the body ideals involved in the subcultural settings of hard-core bodybuilding have, to a certain extent, been mainstreamed and become more closely connected to hegemonic masculinity. There seems to be an ongoing recalibration of the relationship between masculinity and muscle-building. Looking at this from various angles, we have sought a closer understanding of how bodybuilding, steroids, sexuality, and masculinity have been configured in contemporary (fitness) culture.

The ambivalent views of the men in this chapter underscore the tenuous position many (doped) bodybuilders exist in between ideal/deviant bodies. Symbolically, hard-core muscular bodies are regarded as attractive and as expressions of dominance. In media culture, the muscular and defined masculine body is highly valued. Action heroes in the movie industry are usually pumped up, displaying well-defined, sexually attractive, and ripped bodies. Although the narratives here show a certain degree of self-reflection, and an awareness that too much muscularity can be seen as extreme or even deviant, they still worship and value the muscular body. The same goes for the sexual side effects of steroids. Sexual lust and potency are initially and symbolically regarded as core aspects of a vibrant, performance-oriented, heteronormative masculinity. Being able to manage oneself, endure, and to satisfy women is also at the heart of dominant masculinity.

In a broader social context there is more complexity. The men in this chapter are aware that their increased libidos can also be seen as problematic, sometimes as a sign of sex addiction and deviance. There is a delicate balance between sexual and bodily urges and desires on the one hand, and loss of control on the other. Living in a pornographic imaginary can also result in a loss of reasonable contact with the world outside the bodybuilding subculture. In this chapter we have highlighted how this fragile balance between dream and reality – the pornographic imaginary and real intimate relationships – has decisive consequences for the men's relationships. In doing so, we also showed how balance between pleasure and harm may be understood as something of a slippery slope in these men's daily lives. In this way, the pornification of the male body can lead to damaged bonds between the men and their presumptive partners. In fact, upholding this lifestyle and this highly ambivalent construction of masculinity – in between marginality and hegemony – sometimes leads to loneliness and a lack of intimate relationships. The result is a blurring of the lines between fantasy/reality and pleasure/harm. We explore the notions of harm and risk production and mitigation further in the next chapter.

References

Andreasson, J., & Johansson, T. (2021). "Welcome to planet porno." Masculinity, sexuality and fitness doping. *Journal of Bodies, Sexualities and Masculinities, 2*(1), 9-30.

Andreasson, J. (2015). Reconceptualising the gender of fitness doping: Performing and negotiating masculinity through drug-use practices. *Social Sciences, 4*(3), 546–562.

Andreasson, J., & Johansson, T. (2014) *The global gym. Gender, health and pedagogies.* Palgrave MacMillan.

Andreasson, J., & Johansson, T. (2020) *Fitness doping. Trajectories, gender, bodies and health.* Palgrave Macmillan.

Bach. A. R. (2005). *Mænd och Muskler En bog om Stryketæning og Anabole Steroider* [*Men and Muscles A Book about Weight Lifting and Anabolic Steroids*]. Tiderna skrifter.

Begley, E., McVeigh, J., Hope, V., Bates, G., Glass, R., Campbell, J., & Smith, J. (2017). *Image and performance enhancing drugs: 2016 national survey results.* Retrieved January 15, 2020, from: http://ipedinfo.co.uk

Christiansen, A. V. (2020). *Gym culture, identity and performance-enhancing drugs: Tracing a typology of steroid use.* Routledge.

Christiansen, A. V., Vinther, A. S., & Liokaftos, D. (2017). Outline of a typology of men's use of anabolic androgenic steroids in fitness and strength training environments. *Drugs: Education, Prevention & Policy, 24*(3), 295–305. http://dx. doi.org/10.1080/09687637.2016.1231173.

Connell, R. W. (1995). *Masculinities.* Polity Press.

Connell, R. W. (2001). *The men and the boys.* University of California Press.

Copeland, J., Peters, R., & Dillon, P. (2000). Anabolic-androgenic steroid use disorders among a sample of Australian competitive and recreational users. *Drug and Alcohol Dependence, 60*(1), 91-96.

Demetriou, D. Z. (2001). Connell's concept of hegemonic masculinity: A critique. *Theory & Society, 30*(3), 337–361.

Denham, B.E. (2008). Masculinities in hardcore bodybuilding. *Men and Masculinities, 11*(2), 234–242.

Gaines, C., & Butler, G. (1974). *Pumping iron. The art and sport of bodybuilding.* Sphere Books Ltd.

Garlick, S. (2016) *The nature of masculinity. Critical theory, new materialisms, and technologies of embodiment.* UBC Press.

Hambrick, M., Simmons, J., & Mahoney, T. (2013). An inquiry into the perceptions of leisure-work- family conflict among female ironman participants. *International Journal of Sport Management and Marketing, 13*(3/4), 173–199.

Haywood, C., Johansson, T., Hammarén, N., Herz, M., & Ottemo, A. (2018). *The conundrum of masculinity. Hegemony, homosociality, homophobia and heteronormativity.* Routledge.

Hearn, J. (2004). From hegemonic masculinity to the hegemony of men. *Feminist Theory, 5*(1), 49–72.

Howson, R. (2006). *Challenging hegemonic masculinity.* Routledge.

Johansson, T., & Ottemo, A. (2015). Ruptures in hegemonic masculinity: The dialectic between ideology and utopia. *Journal of Gender Studies, 24*(2), 192–206.

Jordan-Young, R.M., & Karkazis, K. (2019). *Testosterone. An unauthorized biography.* Harvard University Press.

Kammeyer, K. C. W. (2008). *A hypersexual society. Sexual discourse, erotica, and pornography in America today.* Palgrave MacMillan.

Kimergård, A. (2015). A qualitative study of anabolic steroid use amongst gym users in the United Kingdom: Motives, beliefs and experiences. *Journal of Substance Use, 20*(4), 288–294. https://doi.org/10.3109/14659891.2014. 911977.

Klein, A. (1993). *Little big men: Bodybuilding, subculture and gender construction.* State University of New York Press.

Locks, A., & Richardson, N. (2012). *Critical readings in bodybuilding.* Routledge.

McCarville, R. (2007). From a fall in the mall to a run in the sun: One journey to ironman triathlon. *Leisure Sciences, 29*(2), 159–173.

McGrath, S., & Chananie-Hill, R. (2009). "Big freaky-looking women". Normalizing gender transgression through bodybuilding. *Sociology of Sport Journal, 26*(2), 235–254.

Monaghan, L. F. (2001). *Bodybuilding, drugs and risk: Health, risk and society.* Routledge.

Mullholland, M. (2013). *Young people and pornography. Negotiating pornification.* Palgrave Macmillan.
Mulrooney, K. J., van de Ven, K., McVeigh, J., & Collins, R. (2019). Commentary: Steroid madness- Has the dark side of anabolic-androgenic steroids (AAS) been over-stated? *Performance Enhancement & Health, 6*(3-4). https://doi.org/10.1016/j.peh.2019.03.001
Parkinson, A. B., & Evans, N. A. (2006). Anabolic androgenic steroids: A survey of 500 users. *Medicine and Science in Sports and Exercise,38*(4), 644-651.
Schwarzenegger, A., & Petre, P. (2012). *Total recall: My unbelievably true-life story.* Simon & Schuster.
Thualagant, N. (2012). The conceptualization of fitness doping and its limitations. *Sport in Society: Cultures, Commerce, Media, Politics*, 15(3), 409–419.
Underwood, M. (2017). Exploring the social lives of image and performance enhancing drugs: An online ethnography of the Zyzz fandom of recreational bodybuilders. *The International Journal of Drug Policy, 39*, 78–85. http://dx.doi. org/10.1016/j.drugpo.2016.08.012

Chapter 6

Anti-Doping: Producing Health or Harm?

The previous two chapters focused on the gendered dimensions of doping, and more specifically on the implications of gender on various forms of risks, side effects, and potential harm from use for both the user and those with whom they have relationships. We will continue this discussion related to risk and harm in this chapter, but the focus will be on different responses to doping that users encounter.[5] We will use two country-specific cases to discuss how anti-doping is understood in relation to strategies that concern prevention and harm-reduction. As we saw in chapters 3, 4, and 5, there are a range of experiences and factors that impact IPED trajectories, use, and use practices. One central factor is the national-level policy that determines the legality of IPED-related behaviors, including use, possession, purchase, and sale of substances. Policy strategies can, to some extent, structure these behaviors, as well as direct broader factors such as what types of resources about use are (un)available, how users acquire substances, and how use is perceived socially. Developing our understanding of how policies and strategies impact different user groups is necessary for identifying points where they may be most vulnerable to risk (i.e., women unable to find reliable information on how to dose substances; learning to inject on one's own) and to determine how to develop more effective interventions. We focus on the risk environments that these different approaches create or mitigate, and in doing so we will also partly return to the contextual divide between sport and fitness doping discussed in chapters 2 and 3.

As noted previously, many fitness dopers have no membership with a governing body comparable to a sports governing body. Individual countries are left to determine their own IPED policies and national laws and approaches to doping in society can vary widely by country (Andreasson & Henning, 2019). Some countries have made doping substances – especially steroids – illegal to buy or sell, while others have criminalized possession and/or use similarly to illicit recreational drugs (European Commission, 2014; FAIR, 2019). In other countries it is also possible to buy and use IPEDs without risk of police interference. In general though, and regardless if we center on the sports or the fitness context, anti-doping responses have largely come to focus on individuals, whether through testing and sanctioning or education and prevention. This focus at the individual and psychological levels has,

---

[5] Parts of this chapter build on an article published in *Drugs: Education, Prevention and Policy* (Henning & Andreasson, 2020)

however, tended to background or even ignore some of the broader environmental factors that work to shape doping behaviors. The risk and reward of doping is to some extent structured by one's environment, which is underpinned by policies related to substance use. As above, these policies may come from WADA or national governments, and may be enforced by NADOs or police authorities (WADA, 2019). Most anti-doping approaches are prohibitive and punitive – they seek to stop the trade or use of IPEDs and punish the individuals involved. We argue that these systems, focused on the individual, may structure the environment so that IPED users are at risk of harm. Fitness and sports, then, can be understood as risk environments (see Henning et al., 2020; Rhodes, 2002; 2009).

This chapter explores two different strategies for addressing doping – prevention and harm reduction – and the tension between the two. We explore the case of Sweden's national prevention-based anti-doping approach and the ways it can contribute to a fitness doping risk environment. We then compare that with the U.K.'s minimally criminalized policy around IPEDs and the harm reduction approach this has allowed in one clinic in Glasgow, Scotland, to understand how these work to enable safer use. We then briefly consider the online enabling environment to understand how IPED users create and engage in virtual community-based harm reduction, as well as the online and offline implications of such an approach. We build on the discussion in the previous two chapters of health and harm in relation to gender and the gendering of IPED use as both a lived experience and a phenonmen. In this chapter, we argue that, together, these environments and approaches both limit and respond to one another while further blurring the lines between promoting health and producing harm.

Risk and Enabling Environments

Work on recreational substance use has considered the ways that many harms of drug use are actually shaped by environmental factors (Rhodes, 2002; 2009). By understanding risk environments – the physical or social spaces where a range of factors converge to increase the chances of drug harms (Rhodes, 2002, p.91) – we can analyze how use behaviors are structured by the anti-doping environment. This brings social, cultural, economic, and policy factors into consideration when looking at doping use patterns and behaviors. Laws prohibiting fitness doping, for example, produce physical risks (i.e., safe supply of substances; dosing knowledge), social risks (i.e., stigmatization as a "doper" or criminal; gendered risks), economic risks (i.e., fines; criminal records visible to potential employers), and policy risks (i.e., criminalization of doping; access to testing services or use equipment). As anti-doping policies for the fitness context can vary widely by country, the specific risks of use change depending on the local environment.

Hegemonic notions of anti-doping derived from sports, however, still permeate these local environments. In some cases, sports anti-doping functioned as the basis for national policies and approaches to IPEDs (Henning & Dimeo, 2018; Møller, 2009).

The overlaps and tensions between sports anti-doping and national laws can, at times, impact the risks local users face (Henning & Dimeo, 2018). Some national anti-doping policies criminalizing use – mostly in the sports context – are in direct conflict with more (neo)liberal laws for recreational or addictive substances. Spain, for example, has criminalized doping while liberalizing its broader approach to drugs for personal use. Other countries have given authority to NADOs for enforcing both sports and fitness doping policies, meaning gym-goers are subject to anti-doping rules in ways similar to elite athletes (Andreasson & Henning, 2019; Christiansen, 2011). These linked policies are further intertwined at the level of enforcement, leading to overlaps in response from athletes and gym-goers.

Harm reduction is a human rights-based approach to reducing the harms caused by drug use, laws, and policies (HRI, n.d.). Organized programs may include needle and syringe exchange programs, substance testing, or supervised use. Some of these programs may now be institutionalized, but harm reduction has its origins at the grassroots level, often operating illegally and without central organization (McLean, 2011). Because of the politicization of drug use, prohibitive laws, and high levels of stigma surrounding use, users themselves intervened to help ameliorate some of the risks of use. While these are mostly associated with recreational drugs, harm reduction strategies have also been introduced for IPEDs (Iverson, et al., 2016; McVeigh et al., 2016).

There are similarities to the grassroots harm reduction approach in the fitness doping context. Determining which substances to use, sourcing a safe supply of drugs, ensuring proper dosing and cycling, learning hygienic use practices, and managing side effects are needs that new users have to address. Some may rely on lay expertise from peers, trainers, or managers at local gyms (Harvey et al., 2020; Kimergård & McVeigh, 2014; Rowe, et al., 2017) – which also may become the site for substance supply – though the level of effective harm reduction in these settings is unclear and may vary (Salinas et al., 2019). These issues can be made even more complex in environments where doping is prohibited and individuals cannot use openly or seek advice from other users in gym or fitness settings (Andreasson & Johansson, 2016). Engaging is some form of DIY harm-reduction is often necessary for IPED users. One place IPED users are likely to turn for information about substances, especially steroids, is online forums (Harvey et al., 2019).

The goal of understanding risk environments is the production of enabling environments. Enabling environments are those that enable (safer) use, often through the introduction and uptake of harm reduction strategies (Rhodes, 2002; 2009). Harm reduction works to reduce the risks across the same physical, social, economic, and policy factors. However, it is not sufficient to create an enabling environment by simply introducing harm reducing measures, nor should these two types of environments be considered separately. There is a dynamic tension between risk and enabling environments, where changes in one are often met with changes in the other. An enabling environment relies on the using population to buy into the strategies and for other stakeholders to support the risk reduction strategies. For example, services teaching safer injection practices must also be willing to ensure clients' confidentiality and not report them to enforcement agencies if such services are to effectively reduce harm. Rather than understanding risk and enabling environments separately, then, researchers should consider them as simultaneously co-existing and co-producing one another (Duff, 2010). What they produce, in turn, shapes doping users' behaviors and practices. This becomes clearer when we consider two competing strategies for addressing doping: prevention and harm reduction.

Preventing, Producing, and Reducing Harm

Zero-Tolerance: The Swedish Case and Harm Production

As an anti-doping strategy, prevention seems like a valid and worthwhile approach. If use is prevented, so are the risks and harms that may accompany it. Prevention work has been deployed by sports anti-doping organizations and through national and local policies. However, prevention strategies have been shown to have mixed effectiveness among groups likely to use IPEDs (see Bates et al., 2019), including youth (Goldberg et al., 2003). In this section we look at Sweden's doping prevention program, PRODIS (Prevention of Doping in Sweden) that adopted prohibitive anti-doping messaging and language, and in general how anti-doping has played out in Sweden and been received by users. We show that while Swedish strategies aim to reduce risks of engaging in use through prevention, they also contribute to environmental risk factors by keeping abstinence as the only acceptable outcome. Nonetheless, doping still happens. Prevention policies and strategies can get in the way of support provision for these individuals, as the focus is always on the "clean" or "natural" athlete or gym-goer. This then precludes other seemingly incompatible strategies, such as harm reduction, that may do more to address the realities of the fitness doping landscape.

Sweden's gym and fitness industry is large, with 44% of the population holding a gym membership, the highest proportion of any country in Europe (Westin, 2018). Estimates put the rate of doping among gym-goers at about four percent (Westin, 2018). Fitness doping in Sweden was initially recognized as a social problem in the late 1980s by the Public Health Agency (Statens Folkhälsoinstitut, 2011). Following a 1989 investigation into steroids, hGH, testosterone, and other muscle-building substances that found widespread use, the Swedish Doping Act (1991) was passed to address doping as a public health issue, coming into effect in 1992. This framing enabled the public health authority to take a holistic approach to anti-doping. One effort has brought anti-doping education and prevention efforts into the school curriculum, as high school students receive mandatory education on making healthy choices, including avoiding the use of drugs and IPEDs (Skolverket, 2011).

In Sweden, the Swedish Sports Confederation is the responsible organizing body and NADO, leading on delivering information and organizing educational events around anti-doping. It also collaborates with other organizations specializing in various strategies. PRODIS is a cooperative group of fitness centers, municipalities, and other stakeholders seeking a doping-free gym environment. PRODIS aims to create a set of shared values around doping among all individuals in the gym and fitness context in a way similar to the welfare state (Andreasson & Henning, 2019).

PRODIS uses a community-based approach adapted from a model developed for alcohol use. They work with the Swedish Sports Confederation, advocates, and local police to establish local anti-doping policies for gyms. They employ various educational components aimed at gym managers and fitness trainers, which can ultimately lead to a diploma for promoting doping-free environments and link graduate gyms with one another across municipalities. PRODIS also works with specialist organizations to develop interventions for gym-goers and fitness centers themselves. One of these is a program called 100% Pure Hard Training (100PHT), which aims to prevent doping by highlighting the achievements possible strictly through training. The anti-doping message is simple: just train.

> *100% Pure Hard training* aims to reduce the use and availability of anabolic androgenic steroids and other doping preparations among exercising at training facilities. This is done by training facilities developing long-term preventive work against doping in collaboration with relevant players in the area, especially between the training industry, the police, the National Sports Federation District Sports Association (DF), the County Administrative Board, the municipality and the county council (Renhardtraning.com, n.d.).

PRODIS notes that in a follow-up survey of users of gyms that worked with the 100PHT method between 2010 and 2014, the proportion of men reporting using steroids at any time (lifetime) dropped by more than half, from 4% to 1.7% (Rehnman Wigstad, 2015). It is difficult to determine whether it is PRODIS's work that has contributed to these changes or whether they could be attributed to other reasons (see Bates et al., 2017). However, this survey only included members of gyms that have adopted 100PHT, so members of gyms that have not or individuals who train in private or home facilities were not included. An evaluation of 100PHT comparing members at gyms that employ the program and those that do not found no significant difference in steroid use between groups over the previous twelve months (Westin, 2018).

While the Swedish Doping Act allowed for a national package of anti-doping and prevention, it deviated from public health approaches to substance use in a significant way. This law not only criminalized possession and trade of muscle-building drugs, but went a step further to criminalize use the presence of a substance in the body (Christiansen, 2009; Pederson, 2010). These strategies were aimed at stopping the use of IPEDs through combined prevention (PRODIS) and deterrence (criminal penalties). As the (estimated) four percent rate of doping among gym members indicates, fitness doping clearly has not stopped in Sweden despite the nation-wide and multi-level approach. Policing fitness centers and strict measures to prevent the use of steroids and other IPEDs can, however, reinforce social stigma for those who choose to engage in the practice (Thualagant & Pfister, 2012). One internationally competitive Swedish bodybuilder, Ian, was detained by police officers at his gym. While civil officers guarded him, his bags were searched. Though he only had legal supplements – amino acids and pre-workout energy products – these were confiscated. Further, as the supplements were found in an opened container, the police said that this constituted probable cause and another unit searched his home while he was held in the gym. Ian felt targeted as this was done in view of members of his gym. He reflected on how the perceptions of steroid use are linked with criminality and violence.

> I only had a small maintenance-dose at home at the moment. I was not doing a heavy course at the time. No, but it's illegal but they probably expected to find an AK47 and hand grenades and some really heavy stuff. That would be their hope. (Ian)

Public perceptions and assumptions about steroid use do not necessarily match the experiences of users themselves (Andrews et al., 2005; Christiansen, 2020; Dunn et al., 2014). Some even try to challenge these narratives of dopers as risky drug abusers. Fully aware that IPED use is criminalized, Ian tried to make a clear distinction between what he thinks the police expect and what his actual involvement in IPED use and other criminal activities actually looks like. Another user, Matt, a bodybuilding coach who also sells steroids to athletes, was arrested and held by police for steroid violations in a similar way to Ian. After he was released, however, a police officer asked him to come back into their station to talk with him about the logbooks detailing his steroid use they had found. Though suspicious, he agreed to speak with them.

> So, I went and she met me in reception, the officer. Welcome, she said, with coffee and everything. Then there were three other people there. One from the anti-doping hotline was there and she had all these copies from my journals or logbooks. She asked, 'where did you get this knowledge from? We want to know who you are and why you know all this.' I told them I've been reading and using for some 20 years, that's how. How it really works. Then there was this little man sitting there, also from the doping hotline, and he was pissed off. How could I think this and that. 'You show a distorted picture of how it works,' I said. And he replied, 'yes, but this is a driveway to heavy narcotics.' 'No, it's not,' I said. In what country? Where? I told him that there are some 40 countries in the world where you can buy them at the pharmacy. They don't have problems with steroids concerning this, but in Sweden we do? (Matt)

Although the initial reason, as understood my Matt, was to meet and have an open discussion about user perspectives and practices, the discussion only enabled mutual understanding to a limited extent. The idea that steroid use will lead to other forms of illicit and recreational drug use echoed gateway hypotheses of substance use. These posit that low levels of even legal substance use (i.e., alcohol; sports supplements) leads to use of heavier and more dangerous drugs (i.e., cocaine; steroids). While there is evidence that steroid use is associated with other forms of substance use, no clear causal relationship in either direction has been established (c.f. Dodge & Hoagland, 2011; Gårevik & Rane, 2010; Kanayama, et al., 2018; Sagoe et al., 2015). However, the doping hotline worker's insistence that Matt and his clients are likely to become illicit drug users seems to reflect the view that all forms of drug use are necessarily unsafe and that stopping and preventing steroid use is the way to prevent further social harms. As a result, such views may act as a barrier to seeking professional support for people using steroids. This is consistent with previous research findings that the lack of knowledge and/or views of steroids among service professionals, including medical service providers, may be a barrier to people who use steroids seeking support (Chandler & McVeigh, 2014; Dunn et al., 2016; Pope et al., 2004).

Another steroid user, Olof, who has been a dedicated gym-goer for 15 years, observed that steroids continue to be heavily criminalized relative to other drugs that seem to carry greater risks of mortality.

> I read this state public inquiry, yes, from 2008, I think. I read it and I don't like it. There is so much missing. It's not correct, it's very pro increased penalties and it's not reasonable in relation to other forms of drug use. Narcotics are really producing much more strain on society and the body. Narcotics make people lose their jobs and everything. You can OD [overdose]. To my knowledge, people rarely OD on steroids and die in that sense. (Olof)

Unsurprisingly, one result of heavy criminalization and enforcement in combination with social stigmatization is that use is pushed further underground and IPED users have to use riskier avenues to obtain their drugs. Ian shared his observations of Sweden's approach.

> I think it is really stupid, the way they work on it today. It's like lifting up the rug and sweeping it further in. It's not going to disappear. People will use it [steroids]. But what has happened is that it gets more organized and now you have to go to HA [Hells Angels] to get it. It becomes heavier, and heavier [more criminalized] people or networks dealing with it. (Ian)

Rather than being supplied by other like-minded fitness enthusiasts, IPED users are effectively cut off from local suppliers. Olof also noted this disconnect.

> The more they increase the punishment, the more it gets connected with heavy criminality. It's the same if you want to buy steroids and the dealer asks if you want to have some coke (cocaine) too, if you are up to both things. I mean wouldn't it be better to go to a guy that is into diet supplements, for example? What has happened is that it gets disconnected from training and health. It increases the risks. (Olof)

The links between IPED supply and criminal networks may be the result of use needing to be done in secret due to the risks of discovery (Fincoeur et al., 2015). This works to reduce supply from local sources – who may have also acted as a source of harm reduction – wishing to avoid legal trouble. As Ian and Olof described, this creates a new set of risks from interacting with already criminalized suppliers and networks. It also removes a possible source of expertise for reducing negative physical effects. This then loops back to reinforce the perceived need for criminal penalties, as IPED users are then understood to engage with criminals (Fincoeur et al., 2015).

Sweden's approach is meant to protect public health by preventing, punishing, and treating IPED use. However, a comprehensive zero-tolerance approach leaves no space for harm reduction, and the gap between zero-tolerance and use in spite of it works to produce new risks to users. Strict and widescale anti-doping messaging contributes to IPED users becoming marginalized and connected to recreational drugs and addiction (c.f. Monaghan, 2001). Users may face social stigma and economic penalties if their use is discovered or suspected (Andreasson & Henning, 2019). As users and potential users are met with intolerance, many are left to begin and continue use alone and without support for reducing risks and minimizing harms. Here, the line between health (public) and harm (individual) blurs. In response, many turn to the types of online communities discussed in chapters 3, 4, and 5 for support and advice on safer use – environments that enable doping.

Tolerance: Risk and Harm in the U.K.

Contrary to Sweden, only the supply and sale of steroids is illegal in the U.K. Steroids are illegal to sell without a license, but purchase and possession for personal use is legal, as is importing or exporting if done in person (i.e., not by post) (UK Government, n.d.). There is no similar comprehensive anti-doping approach in the U.K. comparable to Sweden's, as anti-doping work is targeted at organized (elite) sports athletes through UK Anti-Doping. The U.K. also has a network of harm reduction programs and outreach, including syringe and needle exchange programs (NSP) aimed at reducing risks associated with injected substances. The Crime Survey for England and Wales suggested a steroid prevalence rate of .9%, though this is thought to be a low estimate based on the limits of what it captures (ONS, 2015). Studies of U.K. NSP clients showed a dramatic growth in service uptake by steroid users between 1995 and 2015, accounting for more than half of clients in some regions (McVeigh & Begley, 2017).

One example of a harm reduction program is a drop-in IPED clinic in Glasgow, Scotland. The director for this clinic over the last ten years is John Campbell. The clinic serves a diverse population with a range of ages and backgrounds. They have both men and women clients, though John estimates they see approximately ten men per one woman. One of the main services they provide is support for injecting IPEDs, especially steroids. Because possession and use of steroids are legal in the U.K., John is able to work directly with sellers to direct clients into his clinic.

> It's an anonymous, confidential clinic so we don't work with people's names. You can just pop down and see us. We have a very good relationship with most of the steroid dealers in Glasgow. We give them our business cards, so when they have someone new that buys an IPED off them, they'll give him a card and say "if you get down to clinic, John'll give you needles and he'll show you how to inject." So for them that's actually good cause they don't have to stand in the gym or supplement shop and show people how to inject. And they don't have to order injecting equipment either (…) The benefit for us is we can then engage with people at a very, very early stage.

This early intervention is important for ensuring users have support to minimize the risks of injecting as well as those from the drugs themselves, especially as individuals who use steroids have been found to be reluctant to reveal use to or seek support from medical doctors (Pope et al., 2004). Additionally, research has also found a range of risk behaviors among people using steroids and highlighted the need for service providers to have syringe exchange and safer injecting information available (Zahnow et al., 2018). John's observation that they are able to get clients in at an early stage has been found elsewhere in the U.K. A survey of IPED users found that the age of initiation to injected steroids was the same as first accessing NSPs, meaning safer injection practices and clean equipment are probably used from the start, though while suggested this has not been proven (Begley et al., 2017).

In 2012, about two years after the clinic opened, the U.K. changed the law that had allowed steroids to be imported through the postal service. What resulted was a mix of both harm production and opportunities for harm reduction. John described one almost immediate risk producing effect of this change for his clients.

> So at the start of the clinic, a lot of clients we worked with would import pharmaceutical products, pharmaceutical steroids mainly. So, there was consistency in product and there was obviously good quality control within that. But there were other benefits as well, mainly that they were dosed at a much lower level (...) You didn't see the more obscure veterinarian type substances because pharmacies weren't producing Trenbolone or anything

> (…) So it tended to be testosterone type products at a sensible dose. When they started to tighten up the regulations and made it illegal to import steroids through the mail system even for personal use, then I think it was a bit of a golden handshake to the underground labs as they started producing more underground products and they started competing with each other. So we started seeing higher concentrations (…) So I don't think it was the smartest move, to be honest.

The new criminal policy unintentionally worked to shut off the supply of safer, lower dose drugs and created a new market for unlicensed labs to fill. Often playing on the notion of more is better, these labs began producing very high dose steroids that then altered the expectations of buyers, including among inexperienced users. However, these higher doses also present more risk of unwanted and harmful side effects. Harm reduction services responded to these and other risks of steroid use with new services.

> A lot of stuff we do is safer injecting, you know kind of real time demonstrations, if you like. But what is central to running the clinic are blood tests. So we run a very comprehensive set of bloods post-cycle (…) the blood tests are so powerful, so powerful. You know for encouraging people to stop using altogether, or to encourage them to take a longer period of time off, or to change the drugs they're gonna use on the next cycle.

John found that the introduction of blood tests provided a tool that allowed them to influence clients' behaviors. These were an opening for him to have discussions around "less is more" approaches, encouraging lower doses that would lead to similar muscular development as higher doses but with fewer negative effects. By clearly indicating the physiological effects the drugs are having, John is able to counsel clients away from riskier patterns of use and, at times, to stop completely. Though they do no overt prevention work, some preventative measures are part of the overall harm reduction approach of the clinic. It is important to note here that services such as blood testing and monitoring are rather unique to this clinic – as is John's knowledge and advice – as many services accessed by those using IPEDs across the U.K. offer a much narrower range of services and advice (i.e., NSPs that offer only sterile injection equipment). Further, while John's anecdotal evidence posits this type of service is beneficial, there are no independent evaluations of such services' ability to reduce risk or alter client behaviour. Steroid use behaviour is complex and interventions must take multiple factors into account to be effective. This was highlighted by a socioecological framework by Bates et al. (2019) that took external factors and men's steroid use motivations into account, in effort to inform interventions among this group.

Though many in the IPED community detach their use from that of recreational drug users – an understanding shared by Swedish people who use IPEDs though not within Swedish public discourse on IPEDs (Andreasson & Johansson, 2020; Mullen et al., 2020) – research has found that those who use IPEDs may still stigmatized as drug users (see Harvey et al., 2020; Zahnow et al., 2017), including in other parts of the U.K. (Hanley et al., 2017). However, John has observed how U.K. users may still be stigmatized for the method of use, even leading some to avoid injecting.

> There's a real stigma surrounding using steroids, particularly if it's injected. But we know that people will have to pluck up the courage to go into a pharmacy to ask for needles. That's the benefit of the clinic, to know that judgement isn't really there. Stigma can come from different sources. So if I was a semi-professional rugby player using steroids, I'd be viewed as a cheat. But you wouldn't be viewed as a cheat if you were a bodybuilder (...) Injecting carries the biggest stigma so that's maybe why we see more young people using oral steroids.

This highlights the power of anti-doping narratives in shaping how IPEDs and IPED users are viewed across contexts and countries. Though normalized in some fitness subcultures and even allowed under U.K. law, IPED users still understand their use is not broadly socially accepted. Fear of judgement may work in ways similar to fear of criminal penalties and prevent users from accessing resources that can reduce harm. Clinics and clinicians like John operating with a non-judgmental approach to use are able to counteract some of the environmental risks to use. They are able to intervene because the focus of that clinic is on accepting use and enabling safer practices. One drawback to this approach may be the lack of clear opportunities for prevention work ahead of initiation, though as above, there are elements of prevention within the service.

DIY Harm Reduction: Online Communities[6]

Given the intolerance of IPEDs generally, and in criminalized contexts specifically, it is not surprising that alternative ways of investigating and accessing IPEDs have emerged and a global subculture around use has developed. In the context of online communication, people interested in fitness doping can, for example, anonymously learn about IPEDs and discuss their own experiences without fear of recrimination (Andreasson & Johansson, 2016). These communities often become a repository for collective ethnopharmacological expertise (Monaghan, 2001; Sverkersson et al., 2020). In many ways, these create a virtual enabling environment for IPED use, as it is not only tolerated but supported, normalized, and often oriented towards risk reduction. As we saw in previous chapters, strategies for avoiding or counteracting

[6] Parts of the argument presented in this section builds on a previous paper published in the journal of *Sport in Society* (Andreasson & Johansson, 2016).

negative side effects while maximizing sought for effects are the basis of many discussions in IPED forums.

While many aspects of these communities are geared towards a type of harm reduction, there are still risks to users relying on these sites to guide their use practices. Much expertise is self-declared, meaning most have no formal training or education about health or substance use. Though many are quite knowledgeable, the quality of advice can vary depending on who is giving it out and distinguishing good advice from bad can be tricky for new users. There is often little opportunity for prevention due to the supportive culture around IPED use and the general harm reduction approach. The goal of these forums is not to stop or prevent use, but to enable effective use. Though that may sometimes include delaying or reducing a dose, the community is still one centered around use practices. Together, this may lead to an exaggerated view of how normal or widespread is IPED use, as well as how necessary it is in order to make progress towards fitness goals. As we discussed in chapter 4, these spaces are also often male dominated and male-centered and can exclude women's voices and experiences, including their accumulated knowledge and how it is implemented.

It is also important to consider the impacts of online engagement in the offline context. Use may be discussed online, but the physical realities and personal consequences of it are experienced in the offline world. For example, users may face legal consequences if discovered where use is criminalized, such as in Sweden. In other contexts, such as in the U.K., acquisition is done in a face to face setting, opening up risks for sellers who may face criminal penalties and buyers who must rely on local sellers who may or may not have appropriate products for their needs. The line between online/offline is further blurred once these offline experiences begin making their way back online in the form of cycle logs, commentary, and further advice then passed onto other users. In this way, the online experience informs offline use that then re-informs the online in a kind of circular pattern.

We can see this in two clear examples of the crossover between online advice and offline experience from a Swedish online forum where IPED use and related issues are often discussed. The first is related to avoiding detection when purchasing steroids online.

> We start with the bank transfer. Do not use your internet bank. If your providers get caught and the police go through their accounts, they'll easily find your transaction. (…) Ok, so the question is how to send money. By mail. Preferably use a padded envelope. Fold the money in something before placing it in the envelope – for example, stiff paper or foil or the like, so that no one can see what the envelope contains. (Mailman)

This post was followed by hundreds of replies, indicating the utility of such information within Sweden's criminalized context. Mailman then followed this post with another that contained a checklist for safe purchase: only use encrypted email, delete emails after reading and sending, delete any names, and get rid of any paper receipts from the post office. This is a fairly comprehensive set of instructions for minimizing the legal risks of buying IPEDs on the internet. Though this is useful for offering guidance and support for safer purchasing online, it also underscores the underground and individualized nature of IPED procurement in the offline world as a result of the prohibitive environment. Posts like these not only challenge the policies against IPEDs, but also work to reduce potential social, legal, and economic harms to the individual.

The second example is related to managing the side effects of IPED use. Many users, especially those new to IPEDs, will ask questions related to the negative effects others have experienced and that they may expect. Some of this centers on risk evaluation of use to understand the likelihood of severe effects. One user posted the question "How dangerous are steroids, and could you die?" One of the responses drew on the user's own experiences to warn against some riskier practices.

> One thing is that you're supposed to not overdo it and dribble too much with doses. The risks become far higher then. For a while I was completely wild, and mixed loads of different steroids. Today I only do testo, that's all, and I feel pretty good about it. The only thing I'm not so happy with is the hair on the back and a few other things. (Don'tOverdo)

Don'tOverdo's use of his own experiences shows how knowledge acquired offline can then make its way back online to potentially inform other's use. Don'tOverdo included a chart showing his personal use (substances, doses) to indicate a safer way of using than he had engaged in previously. Other members responded with warnings of other possible side effects, up to and including death, that can result from poor use management, as well as advice on how to recognize early warning signs of negative effects and how to deal with them.

Both Mailman and Don'tOverdo are disseminating knowledge to their online community with the purpose of reducing risks to other users. Use is enabled and normalized in the online context, supported by open discussion and knowledge sharing. However, the recipients of this advice must still act in a prohibitive and punitive offline context. Experience and management of these risks then circles back online in the form of new use logs, updated advice, and further dissemination. Much like the trajectories described in Chapter 3, users slide back and forth between contexts. The result is that what happens in one informs the other in a repeating loop of facing and reducing risk.

Conclusion

Considering two different use environments – zero-tolerance prevention in Sweden and harm reduction in the U.K. – there are clear ways that each approach structures use behaviors and impacts the experiences and possibly the trajectories of IPED users.

The outcomes within and between these differing contexts and approaches highlights how individuals and communities respond to environmental constraints around IPEDs. Restrictive anti-doping environments produce a range of risks for users and may prevent harm reduction. Less restrictive environments may allow for more harm reducing work, but the remaining prohibitions may still produce social, economic, and policy risks. Users in both cases may respond by going to a third environment – the online world – almost completely oriented around reducing harm and enabling use. In some ways, these online communities have developed in response to strict laws, prohibitions, and stigma around IPEDs. Here, users can learn about, discuss, and share their own experience with IPEDs in a low-risk way due to the anonymous nature of many online forums. However, the offline use of these substances are no less risky than use in any other local context. The substances still carry physical risks and the social, economic, and policy risks of the local environment still apply.

There are a range of policy approaches to IPEDs in countries around the world and countries may have more than one relevant law. As we noted in chapter 2, the U.S. initially regulated steroids in response to the Ben Johnson scandal through the Anabolic Steroid Control Act of 1990 (ASCA, 1990). This was updated in response to the Major League Baseball steroid scandal in 2004 (ASCA, 2004) and then again in 2014 to include designer steroids (DASCA, 2014). Since then, the U.S. has also passed a law that allows prosecution of doping organizers or facilitators at events outside the U.S. (RADA, 2019). Similarly, China added to its anti-drug law in 2020 to criminalize doping and instigating doping both domestically and internationally (Garg, 2020). On the other hand, Portugal decriminalized personal possession of drugs in 2001 (Hughes & Stevens, 2010), but athletes are still subject to WADA rules. Each policy will structure the environment and impact users differently, some by design and some not. Understanding these and the role they play in trajectories, behaviors, experiences, and perceptions of use is central to our understanding of more effective interventions. The cases of Sweden and the U.K. used here, however, seem to point to clear implications for IPED users.

Policies targeted at individuals, such as criminalizing sale, purchase, possession, and/or use, have had clear unintended effects at the environmental level and resulted in risks for users beyond those stemming from use itself. This anti-doping risk environment has become formative for IPED practices in ways that are likely in direct opposition to what was intended. However, we can see how the introduction of harm reduction strategies can take various forms depending on what is allowed in the local setting. Absent formal harm reduction services, users themselves find ways to respond and push back against restrictions to enable their own use, such as through the online context. Formal harm reduction focused on user health and needs offers an environment in which safer use is supported and promoted. Moving away from macro-level approaches focused on policing and punishment and towards acceptance and support offers benefits not only for individuals, but it can also have enduring benefits for public health.

REFERENCES

Andreasson, J., & Henning, A. (2019). Glocal fitness doping: Policy, practice and prevention in the United States and Sweden. *Performance Enhancement & Health, 6*(3-4), 103-110.

Andreasson, J., & Johansson, T. (2020). Fitness doping: Trajectories, gender, bodies and health. Palgrave Macmillan.

Andreasson, J., & Johansson, T. (2016). Online doping. The new self-help culture of ethnopharmacology. *Sport in Society, 19*(7), 957-972.

Andrews, G. J., Sudwell, M. I., & Sparkes, A. C. (2005). Towards a geography of fitness: an ethnographic case study of the gym in British bodybuilding culture. *Social Science & Medicine, 60*(4), 877-891.

ASCA. (1990). Anabolic Steroid Control Act. Public law 101-647.

ASCA. (2004). Amendment to the Controlled Substances Act. Public law 108-358.

Bates, G., Begley, E., Tod, D., Jones, L., Leavey, C., & McVeigh, J. (2019). A systematic review investigating the behaviour change strategies in interventions to prevent misuse of anabolic steroids. *Journal of Health Psychology, 24*(11), 1595-1612.

Bates, G., Tod, D., Leavey, C., & McVeigh, J. (2019). An evidence-based socioecological framework to understand men's use of anabolic androgenic steroids and inform interventions in this area. *Drugs: Education, Prevention and Policy, 26*(6), 484-492.

Begley, E., McVeigh, J., Hope, V., Bates, G., Glass, R., Campbell, J., & Smith, J. (2017). *Image and performance enhancing drugs: 2016 National survey results.* Liverpool John Moores University.

Chandler, M., & McVeigh, J. (2014). *Steroids and image enhancing drugs 2013 survey results.* LJMU Centre for Public Health.

Christiansen, A. V. (2020). *Gym culture, identity and performance-enhancing drugs: Tracing a typology of steroid use.* Routledge.

Christiansen, A. V. (2011). Bodily violations: testing citizens training recreationally in gyms. In M, McNamee., & V, Møller. (eds.). *Doping and anti-doping policy in sport,* (pp. 137-152). Routledge.

Christiansen, A. V. (2009). Doping in fitness and strength training environments: Politics, motives and masculinity. In V. Møller, M. McNamme, & P. Dimeo (Eds.), *Elite sport, doping and public health.* University Press of Southern Denmark.

DASCA. (2014). Designer Anabolic Steroid Control Act. Public law 113-260.

Dodge, T., & Hoagland, M. F. (2011). The use of anabolic androgenic steroids and polypharmacy: a review of the literature. *Drug and Alcohol Dependence, 114*(2-3), 100-109.

Duff, C. (2010). Enabling places and enabling resources: New directions for harm reduction research and practice. *Drug and Alcohol Review, 29*(3), 337-344.

Dunn, M., Henshaw, R., & McKay, F. H. (2016). Do performance and image enhancing drug users in regional Queensland experience difficulty accessing health services? *Drug and Alcohol Review, 35*(4), 377-382.

Dunn, M., McKay, F. H., & Iversen, J. (2014). Steroid users and the unique challenge they pose to needle and syringe program workers. *Drug and Alcohol Review, 33*(1), 71-77.

European Commission. (2014). *Study on doping prevention: A map of legal, regulatory and prevention practice provisions in EU 28.* Publications Office of the European Union.

FAIR. (2020). *Fair-Forum for Anti-doping in Recreational Sport 2019. Final report.* Europe Active.

Fincoeur, B., Van de Ven, K., & Mulrooney, K. J. (2015). The symbiotic evolution of anti-doping and supply chains of doping substances: How criminal networks may benefit from anti-doping policy. *Trends in Organized Crime, 18*(3), 229-250.

Gårevik, N., & Rane, A. (2010). Dual use of anabolic-androgenic steroids and narcotics in Sweden. *Drug and Alcohol Dependence, 109*(1-3), 144-146.

Garg, R. (2020). China amends criminal laws in latest anti-doping measure. Jurist. https://www.jurist.org/news/2020/12/china-amends-criminal-laws-in-latest-anti-doping-measure/

Goldberg, L., Elliot, D. L., MacKinnon, D. P., Moe, E., Kuehl, K. S., Nohre, L., & Lockwood, C. M. (2003). Drug testing athletes to prevent substance abuse: Background and pilot study results of the SATURN (Student Athlete Testing Using Random Notification) study. *Journal of Adolescent Health, 32*(1), 16–25.

Hanley Santos, G., & Coomber, R. (2017). The risk environment of anabolic–androgenic steroid users in the UK: Examining motivations, practices and accounts of use. *International Journal of Drug Policy, 40*, 35–43.

Harvey, O., Keen, S., Parrish, M., & Van Teijlingen, E. (2019). Support for people who use anabolic androgenic steroids: A systematic scoping review into what they want and what they access. *BMC Public Health, 19*(1), 1024.

Harvey, O., Parrish, M., Van Teijlingen, E., & Trenoweth, S. (2020). Support for non-prescribed anabolic androgenic steroids users: a qualitative exploration of their needs. *Drugs: Education, Prevention and Policy, 27*(5), 377-386.

Henning, A., McLean, K., Andreasson, J., & Dimeo, P. (2020). Risk and enabling environments in sport: Systematic doping as harm reduction. *International Journal of Drug Policy*. Advance online publication. https://doi.org/10.1016/j.drugpo.2020.102897

Henning, A. & Andreasson, J. (2020). Preventing, producing, or reducing harm? Fitness doping risk and enabling environments, *Drugs: Education, Prevention and Policy*, Advance online publication. DOI: 10.1080/09687637.2020.1865273

Henning, A. D., & Dimeo, P. (2018). The new front in the war on doping: Amateur athletes. *International Journal of Drug Policy, 51*, 128-136.

HRI. (n.d.). What is harm reduction? Harm Reduction International. Retrieved from https://www.hri.global/what-is-harm-reduction

Hughes, C. E., & Stevens, A. (2010). What can we learn from the Portuguese decriminalization of illicit drugs? *The British Journal of Criminology, 50*(6), 999-1022.

Iversen, J., Hope, V. D., & McVeigh, J. (2016). Access to needle and syringe programs by people who inject image and performance enhancing drugs. *International Journal of Drug Policy*. May; 31:199-200. doi: 10.1016/j.drugpo.2016.01.016

Kanayama, G., Pope, H. G., & Hudson, J. I. (2018). Associations of anabolic-androgenic steroid use with other behavioral disorders: an analysis using directed acyclic graphs. *Psychological Medicine, 48*(15), 2601-2608.

Kimergård, A., & McVeigh, J. (2014). Variability and dilemmas in harm reduction for anabolic steroid users in the UK: A multi-area interview study. *Harm Reduction Journal, 11*(1), 19.

McLean, K. (2011). The biopolitics of needle exchange in the United States. *Critical Public Health, 21*(1), 71–79.

McVeigh, J., & Begley, E. (2017). Anabolic steroids in the UK: An increasing issue for public health. *Drugs: Education, Prevention and Policy, 24*(3), 278-285.

McVeigh, J., Kimergård, A., Bates, G., Hope, V. D., & Ncube, F. (2016). Harm reduction interventions should encompass people who inject image and performance enhancing drugs. *BMJ, 353*, i1889.

Møller, V. (2009). Conceptual confusion and the anti-doping campaign in Denmark. In V. Møller, M. McNamme, & P. Dimeo (Eds.), *Elite sport, doping and public health*. University Press of Southern Denmark.

Monaghan, L. (2001). *Bodybuilding, drugs and risk: Health, risk and society*. Routledge.

Mullen, C., Whalley, B. J., Schifano, F., & Baker, J. S. (2020). Anabolic androgenic steroid abuse in the United Kingdom: An update. *British Journal of Pharmacology, 177*(10), 2180-2198.

ONS. (2015). *Drug misuse: Findings from the 2014/15 crime survey for England and Wales*. Home Office, Office for National Statistics.

Pedersen, I. K. (2010). Doping and the perfect body expert: Social and cultural indicators of performance-enhancing drug use in Danish gyms. *Sport in Society, 13*(3), 503–516.

Pope, H. G., Kanayama, G., Ionescu-Pioggia, M., & Hudson, J. I. (2004). Anabolic steroid users' attitudes towards physicians. *Addiction, 99*(9), 1189-1194.

RADA. (2019). Rodchenkov Anti-Doping Act of 2019. Public law 116-206.

Rehnman Wigstad, C. (2015). *Uppföljande kartläggning av användning av dopning, narkotika och kostillskott bland gymtränande. En sammanställning av resultat från Norrbottens län, Västernorrlands län, Stockholms län, Örebro kommun, Östergötlands län, Kungsbacka kommun och Kalmar kommun*. STAD/PRODIS.

Renhardtraning.com. (n.d.). 100% ren förklaring av vår metod [100 per cent clean clarification of our method]. PRODIS/Stockholm STAD. Retreived 2021-04-21 at: https://www.renhardtraning.com/var-metod

Rhodes, T. (2009). Risk environments and drug harms: A social science for harm reduction approach. *International Journal of Drug Policy, 20*(3), 193-201.

Rhodes, T. (2002). The 'risk environment': A framework for understanding and reducing drug-related harm. *International Journal of Drug Policy, 13*(2), 85-94.

Rowe, R., Berger, I., & Copeland, J. (2017). "No pain, no gainz"? Performance and image-enhancing drugs, health effects and information seeking. *Drugs: Education, Prevention and Policy, 24*(5), 400-408.

Sagoe, D., McVeigh, J., Bjørnebekk, A., Essilfie, M. S., Andreassen, C. S., & Pallesen, S. (2015). Polypharmacy among anabolic-androgenic steroid users: a descriptive metasynthesis. *Substance Abuse Treatment, Prevention, and Policy, 10*(1), 12.

Salinas, M., Floodgate, W., & Ralphs, R. (2019). Polydrug use and polydrug markets amongst image and performance enhancing drug users: Implications for harm reduction interventions and drug policy. *International Journal of Drug Policy, 67*, 43-51.

Skolverket. (2011). Läroplan, examensmål och gymnasiegemensamma ämnen förgymnasieskola Retrieved 13 May 2020 from https://www.skolverket.se/undervisning/gymnasieskolan/laroplan-program-och-amnen-i-gymnasieskolan

Statens Folkhälsoinstitut [Swedish national institute of public health]. (2011). Dopning i samhället [Doping in society]. Statens folkhälsoinstitut.

Sverkersson, E., Andreasson, J., & Johansson, T. (2020). 'Sis science' and fitness doping. Ethnopharmacology, gender and risk. *Social Sciences, 9*(4), 55.

The Swedish Doping Act. (1991:1969). Dopningslagen. Stockholm, Sweden: Svensk författningssamling SFS.

Thualagant, N., & Pfister, G. (2012). The fight against fitness doping in sports clubs–political discourses and strategies in Denmark. Performance Enhancement & Health, 1(2), 86-93.

UK Government. (n.d.). Drugs Penalties. Retrieved from https://www.gov.uk/penalties-drug-possession-dealing

WADA. (2019). World Anti-Doping Code 2015: with 2019 Amendments. WADA. Retrieved from https://www.wada-ama.org/en/resources/the-code/world-anti-doping-code

Westin, E. (2018). Återrapportering Uppdrag att utveckla arbetsmetoden 100% Ren Hårdträning och samordna nätverket prevention av dopning i Sverige (PRODIS). Retrieved from: https://www.folkhalsomyndigheten.se/contentassets/351436fc2ecf444b8781e28db4ab7840/sammanfattande-slutrapport-100renhardtraning.pdf

Zahnow, R., McVeigh, J., Bates, G., Hope, V., Kean, J., Campbell, J., & Smith, J. (2018). Identifying a typology of men who use anabolic androgenic steroids (AAS). *International Journal of Drug Policy, 55*, 105–112.

Chapter 7

Conclusions

We began this project with the goal of challenging some of the existing boundaries and separations that seem to surround the ways different doping contexts, cultures, and categories have been defined in both research and public discourse. Given the way doping emerged and developed historically, the lines between cultural contexts are anything but clear cut. Self-experimentation and use of IPEDs, for example, have long histories in bodybuilding and professional sports, both of which developed as primarily male domains. There was even more crossover following the early developments of stimulants and synthetic steroid products, as these were widely accepted for a range of social, medical, and military purposes. Their acceptance and use by sports and gym populations was largely ignored and unregulated until the 1970s. Even then, the visible effects of IPEDs were on display through the 1980s. Women began entering the bodybuilding scene and their more muscular appearances slowly gained acceptance over this same period. This was also later revealed as an era of rampant sports doping by both men and women, as well as a time when polarized conceptualizations of gender were being called into question.

As steroid-aided bodies (of men and women) became bigger and more muscular to align with changing body ideals, sports records were broken again and again by athletes using a range of IPEDs. Spectacles – massive bodies, glittering sports events – were accompanied by scandals in the form of high-profile sports doping cases and deaths linked to IPED use. Doping athletes and fitness fanatics were then gradually and increasingly marginalized as new narratives of clean sport and fitness-for-all took hold in the 1990s alongside the vast commercialization of both sectors. For women, this meant that fit and muscular femininities became acceptable, reflecting some of the mainstreaming efforts of the fitness revolution. Critically, this was also when sports began to take a global approach to regulating doping and national laws further restricting muscle-building drugs were passed in several countries. Thus, what this history tells us is that cultural values and ideals have shifted greatly over time. In doing so, they have also impacted how doping as a phenomenon has been understood in various ways. Socio-historical and cultural fluctuations have also shown the overlaps between subcultural sentiments/practices and mainstream/ideals and cultures.

Even though our main focus in this book has leaned towards fitness doping or IPED use generally, we have continuously sought to expand our analysis to show a more complex picture of how doping is experienced and what doping might look like if we lift categorical constraints – or at least try to bracket them, analytically. We did this by centering the experiences and descriptions of IPED users themselves and allowing these to anchor an expanded understanding of doping as a concept, and as transgressive and culturally perforating experiences. These experiences accumulate within individuals and force a continuous cultural/contextual recalibration. As both a practice and a phenomenon, doping, like the bodies it can shape, is not contextually/culturally bound. Divisions such as those drawn between masculine/feminine, sports/fitness, online/offline, and subculture/mainstream overlook how the construction of seemingly separate spheres that work with and against each other shape the experiences of IPED users.

In this final chapter, we look at how these contexts structure environments to produce or reduce risks, and how IPED users can both reinforce and challenge categories related to IPED use (masculine/feminine; healthy/unhealthy; mainstream/subcultural). We begin this discussion with some remarks regarding the complexity of doping trajectories within and between various performance cultures.

Complex Trajectories

With few exceptions, research on doping in any context has tended to focus on individual-level factors to explain why a person would use IPEDs. These are often underpinned by narrow conceptualizations of motivations and characteristics of likely dopers in a single context: athletes concerned about winning are sports dopers, young men trying to achieve acceptable masculinity are fitness dopers. Such models are useful for showing some general patterns motivating use within specific contexts. However, they flatten our understanding of the paths leading to or away from doping. They also ignore the connections, experiences, and broader socio-cultural environments and structural processes that inform decisions and behaviors leading to IPED use (Andreasson & Johansson, 2020). Attempts to oversimplify these experiences or capture them in a two-dimensional image misses out on the twisting, sometimes circular routes to starting, continuing, or stopping IPED use that can unfold over months, years, or decades through the process of cumulative recalibration. These routes can cut back and forth between contexts as motivations, lifestyle, and interests evolve. This advancement is informed by multi-level factors and processes, from the most personal and individual to very broad social systems.

Users' experiences are shaped as they navigate between contexts, environments, and categories. These influence self-identity and decision making, at times creating momentum down a certain path or towards a new juncture. As we have shown throughout this book, the search for an individual doping trajectory that can be neatly contextually situated and bound to distinct motives is doomed to fail. Typologies and theoretical models can only take us so far (cf., Christiansen, 2020). Individuals may make multiple, gradual approaches towards IPEDs before ultimately deciding to initiate use. The way doping is understood, or the meanings attached to the practice, can change over time as new experiences and information are gained and old perspectives are displaced by new ones. Depending on where one is on their own path, doping can be anything from unthinkable, to a possibility, to a legitimate practice – and possibly multiple things at once. In these ways, doping itself must be understood as a process anchored in cumulative experience rather than a contextually fixed practice that can be described as a given route. Throughout our analysis we have used the term trajectory to begin our discussion on doping paths and the complex ways experiences are gained over the course of time and across various contexts. We have traced bodies and experiences with the intent of highlighting not only directionality towards the now, but also a directionality in which the present is given meaning in relation to (and is influenced by) history. We have conceptualized this in terms of *sedimented histories* (Ahmed, 2006). In the present, experiences are used as capital to motivate and sometimes legitimate one's position. However, knowledge, expertise, and experience must be recalibrated against new goals and circumstances when moving between contexts or (sub)cultures. Thus, an ongoing process of *cumulative recalibration* works to justify and legitimize use. Ideals and lifestyles provide directionality and values are transferable. We can, for example, see how some users in subcultural contexts used various means to relocate their practices when experiencing condemnation by connecting them to neoliberal values, healthism, and processes of medicalization. As such, the practice is disloged from subcultural contexts (sports and fitness) and relocated to mainstream culture and the cult of the individual.

Centering narratives of how individual experiences led to use of IPEDs revealed how some individuals can have multiple and, at times, competing goals, motivations, and views about doping. Athletes may want to perform better in their sports while simultaneously shaping their bodies; fitness users may decide to take up a new sport. Consequently, experiences are played out in a spatiality between contexts. That social capital from one context (sport) can be deployed by users into another (fitness) and is accepted as legitimate currency within the doping subculture also indicates some understanding among members that the lines between sport/fitness and subculture/mainstream are more tenuous than is often acknowledged. In the same way that various forms of capital work across contexts, mainstream notions of acceptable IPED use may also accompany these movements. Such challenges force the individual, as well as other members of the community, to confront these perceived contextual divisions and to renegotiate their own views and justifications for use.

(Re)Negotiating Gender

Online forums have become a space for IPED users, including women, to engage with one another in a collective ethnopharmacological project. These forums can open up new topics to a range of voices and experiences, though they are still spaces where power relations and notions of expertise are contested, including along gender lines. Women have to negotiate gender in both sports and fitness, partly owing to these traditionally having been exclusively male and masculine arenas. Doping is similarly linked with notions of masculinity, both socially and in academic literature on the topic (Christiansen, 2020; Zahnow et al., 2018). In many ways, our understandings of both fitness and doping are rooted in the male experience and tied to patterns of hegemonic masculinity, serving to culturally and individually background and obscure women's experiences and voices. Indeed, women's doping outside of bodybuilding has been largely understudied. This has worked to trap the perspectives and practices of women who use IPEDs between male-dominated accounts of muscles and masculinity and the more individualized, health-focused fitness revolution that reinforces forms of physical femininities adhering to the notion of emphasized femininity (see Smith Maguire, 2008). Women who build muscles and use IPEDs present a challenge to traditional notions of (physical) femininity, although it is only culturally accepted to a certain degree, after which women hit a muscular ceiling of sorts (Dworkin 2001). Still, according to Butler (1998) women's sport has the power to rearticulate gender ideals and norms that at times have been considered outside the norm but are gradually becoming constitutive of a new ideal (see also Tredway, 2014). This also means that norms of what doping can mean when women and women's bodies are foregrounded begin to change. However, women must first negotiate the spaces where these meanings are made and remade.

Beyond centering male bodies, conversations about doping are often dominated by male voices. As in the "Women and Steroids" forum, women and their experiences and use were the topic, but men were often the discussants. This filtered information for and about women through men's knowledge and perspectives of women and, at times, drowned out women's own voices and experiences. Women had to navigate around the men spreading into this space in order to find and engage with other women (Henning & Andreasson, 2019). One potential remedy lies in creating new women-only spaces. By excluding men, women have the opportunity to claim a space where there is potential to build their own collective knowledge based in their embodied experiences; inclusion by exclusion, in a way. There is also the possibility that women in these exclusive spaces can sever the tie between gendered discourses of muscularity and IPED use, thus reforming the environment and potentially altering women's experiences and relationships with IPEDs. This may lead to new links between women's IPED experiences and medical, health, and harm reduction discourses. More importantly, new forms of engagement in women-only spaces may impact women's trajectories to and from IPEDs, as their interactions and what it means to be a doping woman are reimagined and remade.

However, this breaking and remaking is unlikely to be clear or straightforward, especially as women move between the online and offline "worlds." The women who engage in these forums also face offline pressures and expectations around gender. Even women who do not seek to achieve the type of femininity marketed as ideal within the fitness industry are still confronted with it. Indeed, women can be aware of the limited bounds of expected femininity and still wish to achieve a muscular body. While women may have more space and freedom to create their own narratives in places like women-only forums, their lived experiences may differ. How they negotiate these demands – by embracing other ways of performing femininity or continuously challenging emphasized femininity – is likely to be a mix of disputing and upholding hegemonic gender patterns.

Despite their dominance in the fitness world and traditional links between men, muscles, virility, and steroids, male dopers must also navigate issues of gender and sexuality both in the gym and in their daily lives. Hyper-muscular bodies – often built with the help of steroids and other muscle-building drugs – have been brought into the mainstream to some extent. Increased exposure to physiques that were previously relegated to basement gyms and competition stages through popular culture (e.g., comic book heroes, action films, etc.) have linked them more closely with hegemonic masculinity. This brings with it a set of expectations and values that impact how male bodybuilders understand their bodies and engage with others as they navigate the line between marginal and hegemonic demonstrations of masculinity. Hard-core muscular bodies are considered symbols of sexual attractiveness, heteronormative virility, power, and control. The bounds of acceptability of these bodies are less clear, however, and there is some awareness that too much muscularity can cross over into deviance.

Other traits are more complex still, especially when considering the sexual side effects of steroids. Men who are able to out-perform sexually are desirable and enjoy a pleasurable effect of steroid use, fulfilling a fantasy attached to hegemonic conceptions of masculinity. This sexual prowess is valued but only to a limited extent. Men who engage in too much sexual activity or with too many partners may be marginalized as sexual deviants unable to control their physical urges and desires for sex. This reality can have important consequences for men's personal lives and relationships, as the need for and pursuit of excess amounts of sex can undermine or harm prospects for deeper bonds with (potential) partners and lead to isolation from the more mainstream world. Male steroid users, then, must engage in a balancing act where their lifestyle goes beyond the hegemonic but does not quite reach a marginalized masculinity.

Creating Contexts, Producing Risk

Doping is a unique issue in that it is often defined as much by the response to it – specifically anti-doping – as it is by the actual process or practice (see Waddington & Smith, 2009). IPED use is regulated at multiple levels (i.e., local, global) and by multiple policymaking bodies (i.e., WADA, national governments, sports federations/leagues). WADA's establishment had a widespread effect on views and regulations of doping, fueling intolerance of IPEDs beyond sports. WADA's early focus on elite athletes and its mission of ensuring doping-free sports has been widely accepted. The WADA Code has hundreds of signatories from sports organizations and the UNESCO International Convention Against Doping in Sport has been ratified by 187 states, under which member countries agree to align with WADA's policies and standards. The broad acceptance by sport stakeholders and most countries has led to a widespread condemnation of doping in sports, especially in the wake of highly visible scandals and narratives around doping as part of a "win at all costs" sports culture. In many ways, this has linked the notion of doping with cheating, un-sportsperson-like behavior, and other forms of corruption. As gym-goers are not governed by anti-doping unless they belong to a WADA signatory organization, use outside of sport is largely regulated by national laws that may or may not be attached to sports anti-doping work. This means laws and enforcement vary outside of sport, such as the differences between Sweden and the U.K., but also that the sports context and the fitness context are generally treated separately at the policy level. This distinction has become entrenched and doping is usually understood only in relation to a singular either/or context.

No matter the specific policies or approaches, IPED use still occurs. These approaches do, however, create the varying conditions in which use happens and structure the use environment in ways that direct doping behaviors. They can also blur the line between producing/reducing harms, at times working against their own goals. Intolerant and criminalized approaches, such as in Sweden, can push use and users into situations that increase their vulnerability (i.e., engaging with criminal networks, unsafe supplies) when prevention and deterrence fail. This leads to physical risks of unsafe use, but also social, economic, and policy risks arising from detection. Zero-tolerance approaches are meant to prevent harm by eradicating use but can cross over into producing new harms as IPED users find alternative ways of engaging in use. Rather than eradicate use, it can socially marginalize users. Conversely, harm reducing interventions, such as needle and syringe exchange programs, can alter the environment so that safer use is enabled. The U.K.'s hybrid approach – criminalized postal importing and trafficking, legal possession and use – produces harms associated with criminalization, but also minimizes others with a public health-informed harm reduction strategy for users.

Punitive policies and approaches may drive users or potential users into online doping spaces. Users join these online communities in order to learn about IPEDs and their use behind the veil of anonymity offered by many such forums that are unavailable offline (Andreasson & Johansson, 2016). Others may engage to gain and share experiences and information around IPED use (Monaghan, 2012; Sverkersson et al., 2020). Many virtual doping spaces seek to enable use through their general acceptance of use and harm reducing orientations to IPEDs. These forums and discussions contribute to the development of a bank of expertise and experience, especially around harm reduction strategies, and can enable safer use within these IPED user communities. Several risk factors in the local environment linked to detection can be reduced by engaging online. There are, however, accompanying shortfalls in an environment that embraces and normalizes IPED use: potentially poor or misguided advice, lack of prevention, and mismanagement of side effects. These are all potential harms that can have consequences in the offline, physical world. Though these risks apply to the general population of online IPED users, as above, women face a unique set of challenges within both online and offline doping subcultures.

Doping in Transition

Doping is in transition, both in terms of how individuals experience and engage in the practice and how researchers conceptualize doping itself. In order to better understand these transitions, we have attempted to blur the contextual, cultural, and categorical barriers that prevent a broader understanding of the meanings and bodies at the center of the practice. We have shown how contexts and categories themselves may not be so fixed. Gender norms and notions of masculine/feminine are undergoing new challenges as more women emerge and claim space as active participants within doping subcultures. These new voices have the potential to destabilize hegemonic gender patterns and create new, women-centered discourses and narratives of doping. The lines between online/offline, healthy/unhealthy, and mainstream/subcultural are further smudged as users engage and exist in each/all simultaneously, carrying knowledge, information, and values across and between that shape behaviors, decisions, use, and risks. As individuals cycle between and around these contexts, they can begin to shift perceptions of what doping is and, to some extent, its acceptability within various settings and interlinked performance cultures through an ongoing process of *cumulative recalibration.* Further, we have called into question categories of producing/reducing harm to show how the policy environment can impact the levels of risk users face.

Importantly, we argue that there are multiple ways to understand doped bodies and that we must approach these as a question of both/and. By decontextualizing doping, we have shown how doping, and the meanings and values attached to it, change as individuals shift back and forth between contexts and move along routes towards and away from the practice. As bodies move and change, doping practices and perspectives may be challenged, examined, and re-formed in ways that align with current goals and lifestyles to allow the next transition. These movements can blur the lines often drawn around various doping related notions in effort to distinguish one type of use from another. Taking this broader view, we can see that there are overlaps that allow an individual to exist and engage with doping within and between multiple contexts (sports/fitness; mainstream/subcultural; online/offline) simultaneously. As such, doping is no longer something we can understand as contextually fixed – doping is a dynamic process that can be bent and molded to fit new realities emerging over time. Only through contesting such divisions and seeking to move beyond them can we develop a three-dimensional understanding of doping and those who engage with it.

REFERENCES

Ahmed, S. (2006). *Queer phenomenology. Orientations, objects, others*. Duke University Press.

Andreasson, J., & Johansson, T. (2020). *Fitness doping: Trajectories, gender, bodies and health*. Palgrave Macmillan.

Andreasson, J., & Johansson, T. (2016). Online doping: The new self-help culture of ethnopharmacology. *Sport in society: Cultures, commerce, media, politics, 19*(7), 957–972.

Butler, J. (1998). *Athletic genders: Hyperbolic instance and/or the overcoming of sexual binarism*. Stanford Humanities.

Christiansen, A. V. (2020). *Gym culture, identity and performance-enhancing drugs: Tracing a typology of steroid use*. Routledge.

Dworkin, S. (2001). "Holding back": Negotiating a glass ceiling on women's muscular strength. *Sociological Perspectives, 44*(3), 333-350.

Henning, A., & Andreasson, J. (2019). "Yay, Another Lady Starting a Log!": Women's Fitness Doping and the Gendered Space of an Online Doping Forum. *Communication & Sport*. Advance online publication. https://doi.org/10.1177/2167479519896326

Monaghan, L.F. (2012). Accounting for Illicit Steroid Use. Bodybuilders' Justifications. In A, Locks., & N, Richardson. (eds.) *Critical Readings in Bodybuilding*. Routledge.

Smith Maguire, J. (2008). *Fit for consumption: Sociology and the business of fitness*. Routledge.

Sverkersson, E., Andreasson, J., & Johansson, T. (2020). 'Sis science' and fitness doping. Ethnopharmacology, gender and risk. *Social Sciences, 9*(4), 55.

Tredway, K. (2014). Judith Butler redux the heterosexual matrix and the out lesbian athlete: Amélie Mauresmo, gender performance, and women's professional tennis, *Journal of the Philosophy of Sport, 41*(2), 163-176, DOI: 10.1080/00948705.2013.785420eview, 6, 103-111.

Waddington, I., & Smith, A. (2009). *An introduction to drugs in sport. Addicted to winning?* Routledge.

Zahnow, R., McVeigh, J., Bates, G., Hope, V., Kean, J., Campbell, J., & Smith, J. (2018). Identifying a typology of men who use anabolic androgenic steroids (AAS). *International Journal of Drug Policy, 55*, 105–112.

Appendix: Methods and Data

This book is the outcome of two different research projects that we, Jesper Andreasson and April Henning, have been involved in over the past couple of years. In this appendix, we will present a short note on the methods used in these projects, and, as a means for transparency, also explain our approach to data and fieldwork. Although the empirical material used in this book comes from different projects, it is worth emphasizing that in the presentation the findings have been guided by a shared overall purpose, as outlined in chapter 1. The scope of data collection strategies should consequently be understood as a form of methodological triangulation intended to expose "unique differences or meaningful information that may have remained undiscovered with the use of only one approach or data collection technique" (Thurmond 2001, p. 255). The projects from which we built are, first, a longitudinal ethnography and, second, a netnographic study of online IPED communities. Additionally, we have also used a few case studies when finalizing the book, as described below.

Longitudinal Ethnography

One large dataset that has been used emanates from a longitudinal ethnography that was conducted by one of the authors (Jesper), and in which 30 Swedish fitness dopers were followed over the course of several years. Participants were strategically selected, based partly on demographic variables and social position (class, gender, ethnicity, and age), and partly on their different exercise habits and interests in the gym, in addition to their experience with doping substances. Fieldwork typically entailed interviews, direct observations, and informal conversations in the everyday life of fitness dopers.

The interviews were mainly conducted using a biographical approach (Shamir et. al., 2005; Merill & West, 2009; Hallqvist & Hydén, 2012). We were interested in following different social and cultural trajectories through storytelling and the ordering of important life events. The first set of interviews were semi-structured and mainly retrospective. Questions focused on specific themes, such as training background and experience, initial thoughts about doping, first experience with doping, gender, body, doping laws, experiences of preventative work, and harm-reduction, among other topics. The intention was to leverage the different themes to search for clues about the various processes through which the participants became doping users and how this was understood. Follow-up interviews were less structured and focused on events and issues not fully covered in earlier interviews and observations. Our perspective was that each participant had an individual trajectory in which certain encounters or situations were understood as particularly significant for that person's subsequent progression to doping. As we saw it, it was our job to try to create a mosaic through multiple narratives on doping, reflecting how this practice was understood and experienced by users. However, although the interviews initially focused on retrospective narratives that is, their trajectories towards fitness doping we also tried to reflexively investigate how their perceptions of doping use changed in the present.

In order to establish relationships of trust and be able to challenge/validate the interview data, the participants were also followed in their everyday life – for example, in various training situations – using direct observations. The advantage of "direct" observation is that our presence "when and where it happens" yields knowledge that is different from and complementary to the information provided by the participants. The observations gave us an opportunity to contextualize the verbal. It was also beneficial because it made it possible to investigate various aspects of the research settings that might otherwise be forgotten or perceived as trivial (Giddens, 1986; Pink, 2009).

Netnographic Studies on Doping Forums

The second set of data (and project) that has been used for the book emanates from studies of online forums where doping is discussed and debated by users. In this project, we have largely focused on two separate forums and virtual platforms, *Flashback* and *ThinkSteroids*. *Flashback* is hosted in Sweden and although there are the occasional contributions posted in Norwegian, Danish, and English, the posts are mainly in Swedish. The site notes that this is "Sweden's largest forum for freedom of expression, opinion, and independent thinking," and it may be considered a highly open-minded forum with regard to prohibited activities such as the use of IPEDs. *ThinkSteroids* is in many ways similar to *Flashback*, although members communicate in English on this platform. *ThinkSteroids* hosts several different and thematised forums. *ThinkSteroids* (and *Flashback*) are thus divided into different forums around broad topics such as "Steroid News Forum," "Steroid Legal Forum," "Women and Steroids," and so on.

On both *Flashback* and *ThinkSteroids*, and on most online IPED communities, anyone with an internet connection can learn about doping and comment with their experiences and knowledge of doping. Using this type of material has given us access to not only experiences of doping, but also discourses on different drugs and other means of enhancing and changing the body. When conducting our online research, we were inspired by a specially designed method for studying the social web of culture and communities online called netnography. This method, developed by Kozinets (2010), is as the name suggests, methodologically influenced by the traditions and practices of ethnography, as well as cultural- and social anthropology (Hine, 2000). Undoubtedly, internet-focused methods such as netnography differ from conventional ethnographies (see above). For example, online posts cannot easily be positioned in certain geographic places. Further, this kind of study only grants the researcher a limited ability to gather data from offline events as it generally excludes face-to-face interaction (Hooley, et al., 2012). At the same time, it can be noted that internet research methods have similarities with other, more traditional qualitative methods. Online communities are, for example, usually themed in ways that will attract and target specific audiences and groups of people (Orgad, 2006). Therefore, they may appear to be embedded in a particular socio-cultural and/or national context, although not bound by such. Adding to this, social practices on the internet have blurred the boundaries between public and private and made personal information more easily accessible than ever before, thus creating new opportunities for interaction and lifestyle choices (Joinson, et al., 2007; Hugh, 2010). As Kozinets concluded:

> With our ideas and actions, we choose technologies, we adapt and shape them. To this realisation it is also critical to add that our culture does not entirely control the technologies that we use, either. The way that technology and culture interact is a complex dance, an interweaving and intertwining. This element of technocultural change is present in our public spaces, our workplaces, our homes, our relationships and our bodies – each institutional element intermixed with every other one. Technology constantly shapes and reshapes our bodies, our places, and our identities, and is shaped to our needs as well. (Kozinets, 2010, p. 22)

Emphasizing the importance of including technology in efforts to understand people's everyday life, Kozinets showed that the study of narratives on the internet can be an excellent source for understanding the construction of cultural meaning. Focusing on texts and images on *Flashback* and *ThinkSteroids*, in this project we took the perspective that internet communications/communities can be viewed, in one way or another, as cultural manifestations that are important for our understanding of doping cultures and experiences (Kozinets, 2010).

Adding to the above projects, we have conducted a few semi-structured qualitative interviews with key respondents who, in one way or another, have in-depth knowledge of doping practices (Yin, 2014). In chapter 6, for example, we focused on narratives gathered from individuals with in-depth knowledge and experience of policies and responses to doping: those are the prevention work being conducted in Sweden and the harm reduction efforts in the U.K. Using case studies representing diverse responses, we gained insights into how different national settings produce enabling and risk environments. In other chapters we chose to present personal portraits of users and their understandings of doping, their trajectories, and how the practice was understood in relation to factors such as gender. These case studies emanated from the longitudinal ethnographic project described above. The contributions of using case studies are, as we see it, that they can allow both highly personal portraits and make it possible to analyze wider structural/cultural patterns, such as how national-level policies and approaches to IPEDs structure use.

Formal ethical approval for carrying out the research has been secured from the Regional Ethical Review Board of the University of Linköping in Sweden (Ref. No. 2017/468-31; 46-09), and the General University Ethics Panel at the University of Stirling, Scotland (No. 1006).

References

Giddens, A. (1986). *The Constitution of Society*. University of California Press.

Hallqvist, A., & Hydén, L-C. (2012). Work transition as told: A narrative approach to biographical learning. *Studies in Continuing Education, 35*(1), 1-16.

Hine, C.M. (2000). *Virtual ethnography*. Sage Publications.

Hooley, T., Marriott, J., & Wellens, J. (2012). *What is online research?* Bloomsbury.

Hugh, M. (2010). New Connections, Familiar Settings. Issues in the Ethnographic Study of New Media Use at Home, In C, Hine. (Eds), *Virtual methods. Issues in social research on the internet* (pp. 129-140), Berg.

Joinson, A., McKenna, K., & Postmes, T. (2007). *Oxford handbook of internet psychology*. Oxford University Press.

Kozinets, R. (2010). *Netnography. Doing ethnographic research online*. SAGE Publications.

Merill, B., & West, L. (2009). *Using biographical methods in social research*. SAGE.

Orgad, S. (2006). The cultural dimension of online communication. A study of breast cancer patients' Internet spaces. *New Media & Society, 8*(2), 877–899.

Pink, S. (2009). *Doing sensor ethnography*. Sage.

Shamir, B., Daya-Horesh, H., & Adler, D. (2005). Leading by biography: Towards a life-story approach to the study of leadership. *Leadership, 1*(1), 13-29.

Thurmond, V.A. (2001). The point of triangulation. *Journal of Nursing Scholarship, 33*(3), 253-258.

Yin, R. (2014). *Case study research. design and methods*. Sage.